INTRODUCTION

Welcome to the world of digital publishing ~ Using state of the art digital technology and equipment, VelocePress is able to bring titles back in print allowing you to access the information that you need, when you need it. Never has information been so accessible and it is our hope that this book serves your informational needs for years to come. While this edition is presented unchanged from the original 1967 edition it has been reproduced using the latest print-on-demand technology.

If this is your first exposure to digital publishing we hope that you are pleased with the results. Many more titles of interest to the classic automobile enthusiast are available via our website at **www.VelocePress.com** we hope that you find this title as interesting as we do.

NOTE FROM THE PUBLISHER

The information presented is also unchanged from the original edition and has not been updated to reflect changes in common practice, new technology, availability of improved materials or increased awareness of chemical toxicity. As such, it is advised that the user consult with an experienced professional prior to undertaking any procedure described herein.

INFORMATION ON THE USE OF THIS PUBLICATION

This manual is an invaluable resource for the Sunbeam Tiger enthusiast and whilst every care has been taken to ensure correctness of information it is obviously not possible to guarantee complete freedom from errors or omissions or to accept liability arising from such errors or omissions. Therefore, by using the information contained within this manual, any individual that elects to perform or participate in do-it-yourself modifications acknowledges that there is a risk factor involved and that the publishers or its associates cannot be held responsible for personal injury or property damage resulting from the outcome of such repairs.

www.VelocePress.com

Sunbeam Tiger Performance Tuning

by Gordon Chittenden

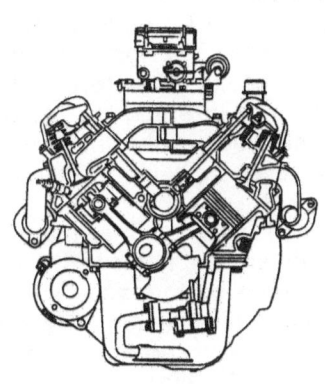

With
A Special "How-To" Section
On Performance Tuning
The Ford 260 cu. in. Engine

COPYRIGHT ©1967 by

FLOYD CLYMER PUBLICATIONS
World's Largest Publisher of Books Relating to Automobiles,
Motorcycles, Motor Racing, and Americana
222 NO. VIRGIL AVE. LOS ANGELES, CALIFORNIA 90004

ANNOUNCEMENT

This informative book on performance tuning the Sunbeam Tiger is authored by Gordon Chittenden. Gordon's Tiger, at the time of writing was American Hot Rod Association National Record holder in its class. This book is therefore, authoritative and based on the author's experience in preparing his own car. A new, outstanding feature of this book is the "How-to" step-by-step photo section which allows even a beginner to undertake the job of tuning the Tiger.

The book tells you how to get maximum performance out of the Ford V-8 260 cu. in. engine. It shows the steps towards making the Tiger into a maximum performance street-use sports car all the way to building up a race winning Tiger for both road races and drag racing events. I am certain you will like this truly fantastic "how-to-do-it" book. Nothing like it has ever been published.

Floyd Clymer

CONTENTS

Acknowledgements 4
Introduction 5
The Basic Engine 7
Initial Performance Tuning 14
Going For Top Performance 23
Induction System 32
Transmitting The Power 35
Chassis Tuning 38
The Custom Tiger 39
Tuning To Win 42
Suppliers Directory 46
Installation Tips — LAT Options 49
Troubleshooting 53
Spark Plug Notes 57
Factory Options 58
Torque Specifications 59
Ribbon Gauge Clearances 60
Holley Hi-Performance Carb 62
Special Parts Numbers 63
Speedometer Corrections 65
The Sunbeam Tiger II 90
Illustrated "How-To" Section 92

ACKNOWLEDGEMENTS

I would like to express thanks to the people who have spent countless hours in helping to develop the Tiger into a first class competitive sports car.

In gratitude to Cliff Brien, Wally Cartwright, Danny Shields, Don Von, Bill Woodul and Ron Root, thanks again.

To Tom Coyne, Service Representative of International Automobiles, Inc., Maurice Howard, Parts Manager of International Automobiles, Inc., and Mr. Richard Wheatly, of Traction Master, my thanks for the help and needed parts. To Shelby-American, Inc., and Ford Motor Co., too, thanks for the hard-to-find technical data.

And thanks to the man who started the Tiger, Mr. Ian Garrad, President of International Motors, Inc.

To Larry Reed, sponsor of one of the winningest Tigers, mine, thanks once more.

Gordon Chittenden

INTRODUCTION

In the summer of 1963, a few owners of what they had thought were rather powerful sedans were shocked when a bright red Sunbeam Alpine appeared in their rear view mirrors, swung to the outside and, with a throaty exhaust foreign to the small four-cylinder engine supposedly under the hood, blasted by, leaving them both astonished and puzzled.

As word of the "Q-ship" Alpine started to spread even as far south as San Diego from Los Angeles, a rumor was also starting to spread, "The Alpine was to get a V-8 engine."

The rumor grew stronger, and those that had heard the rumor were seen in Alpine dealerships looking under the hoods of Alpines; shaking their heads, they would all agree, "They'll never get a V-8 in there."

If you'll look under the hood of an Alpine, chances are you too would agree, getting a V-8 in there isn't easy.

Mr. Ian Garrad, manager of Rootes Motors, West Coast then is rightfully credited with being the father of the Alpine-260, which in production was to become known as the Sunbeam Tiger.

Converting Mr. Garrad's ideas from drawing board to machinery was the responsible task of the late Ken Miles, and the old snake charmer himself, Carroll Shelby.

There were two prototype Tigers in the first few months: one constructed by Ken Miles simply had the V-8 engine "dropped" into it, no alterations of the firewall, just the old hotrodders trick of engine swapping. That one was fitted with a two-speed automatic, and in all honesty wasn't the best handling car on the road, what with considerable weight on the front end and what was then stock Alpine Series III suspension under it, plus small 5.90x13 tires mounted on 4" wide wheels. But it did go like heck in a straight line with its single four-barrel carburetor looking out of place under the hood.

The second prototype, a white one, was being built at the Shelby-American plant, then in Venice; this one had undergone more than just a "drop-in" engine transplant. The firewall had been altered considerably; steering was now rack and pinion. The suspension underwent several running changes until the car was considered suitable for some rather harsh inspection. At this point the red prototype was shipped off to England, and the white one quietly disposed of.

Arriving at the duly appointed time at Coventry, Mr. Garrad presented the Tiger to Lord Rootes, who being an ex-racing driver and a man who would have no part of a hashed up hotrod, would be the final judge as to whether the project would go on from this point or not.

Mr. Garrad went over the technical details of the Tiger, presented a set of performance figures, and Lord Rootes departed in the car for an hour's drive over the English roads.

On returning, the decision was on Lord Rootes' face; a new Tiger was born. Not the first Tiger that had carried the name from Rootes Motors; the first had been built in the 30's for Sir Malcolm Campbell to attack the land speed records.

Over a full year's extensive testing then went into some Rootes-built prototypes, and in April of 1964 the new production Tiger was presented at the New York International Auto Show.

From the prototype that Lord Rootes drove over the English roads some four years ago to the 1967 models, the Tiger has undergone really very little in major changes. The original tail-fins are gone, the folding-top has been improved, and a new fresh-air-intake to the cockpit, slightly lighter steering, and improved suspension rates make up the major changes.

The heart of the Tiger, the V-8, 260 cubic-inch engine rated at 164 B.H.P. @ 4400 r.p.m. is unchanged from the red prototype that alarmed a few drivers on some English roads in 1963.

And this mild mannered heart is nothing to be ashamed of in spite of its mild state of tune as it leaves the dealer's showroom.

The Sunbeam Tiger division of the now Simca/Rootes division of Chrysler Motors has a complete option list that will allow you to set up a Tiger to become a National Record Holder in the American Hot Rod Association, which it currently does, and has held the record for two years; or you can go rallying, as the Factory did at Monte Carlo, and won their class; or, you can go road racing, which the Tiger did at the Riverside Grand Prix in October 1966, and the Tiger won its own class, B/Production, but finished fourth overall as well in the A, B, C production race in full view of over 80,000 paying spectators leaving no doubt who was the **real Tiger.**

This book, then, is not going to tell you how to get economy run mileage from the Tiger, but will show you how to get over 100 additional and honest horsepower out of what was a under-tuned engine to start out with. And the best part of all is that most of the power-increasing parts are available as Sunbeam options!

THE BASIC ENGINE

The Tiger engine in showroom stock condition is a very detuned engine, which when originally installed in the Ford Falcon and Fairlane wasn't the hottest thing on the road.

The engine did however have a lot of untapped performance potential, and this was proven when the same engine that did little in the Falcon was in the Tiger's chassis. Even untouched it is a very fair performer; this is due partly to the fact that the engine now had less weight to haul around, and two, the Tiger is fitted with a very excellent four-speed transmission allowing the driver to make full use of what is at hand.

In stock trim, the engine is rated at 164 H.P. @ 4400 r.p.m.; this is gross horsepower, and the average engine right out of the crate so to speak will actually put out 141 H.P. on an engine dyno.

When the engine is in the car, power, by the time it gets back to the rear wheels, has dropped off quite a bit.

The average showroom stock Tiger will put out often only around 70 H.P. at the rear wheels at 3000 r.p.m., and a maximum of only 94-96 H.P. at the rear wheels @ 4800 r.p.m.

This might seem like an awfully low amount of HP, but remember we are talking about **honest horsepower** on a very accurate dyno.

With a fair amount of tuning, this HP at the rear wheels can be increased up to 128 HP @ 4800 rpm. It is going to take some work to get, though, but not a lot of money.

The best starting point on the Tiger is in the ignition department. The stock distributor is a single point, vacuum & mechanical advance distributor. The stock ignition spark plug wires are the type called "Radio Carbon." This wiring uses a center of carbon in place of solid copper wire; while it is designed to function as a radio resistor type of ignition wire, it is subject to heat breakdown, and often fails at even mid-rpm ranges. The life of this wire is at best very short, and it is totally unsuitable for any form of performance tuning.

Then here we are going to spend the first $10.00, if, that is, you have already purchased the **Sunbeam Workshop Manual** No. WSM-143, (Rootes part No. 6601125) or the Floyd Clymer **Sunbeam Owners Handbook;** if you haven't already got one or the other, stop, do not pass go, do not start to work, go back to the bookstore.

The stock ignition wiring then is going to have to be replaced with a set of high quality solid wire ignition wiring, such as the Packard 440 or AUTOLITE cable.

The use of the AUTOLITE wire will make things easy; a complete kit of pre-cut wires, with the spark plug connectors already installed, is available for $10.00 list. The part number is C5ZZ-12259-A. By the use of this kit it is only a matter of replacing the old with the new; no cutting will be required. Many Sunbeam dealers carry the kit, and all Ford dealers carry it.

We are not talking about the "orange" colored Autolite cable at this time. While it's very good and a requirement for a competition engine, it is also far too expensive for just a street machine. But if you really think you want it, remember it costs about $1.30 per foot! Back to the ten-dollar kit for the time being.

The only important thing to remember when installing the new wire is to pay attention to the routing of the ignition wires to the plugs. They should be routed exactly as shown on page 71 of the Rootes Shop manual, or on page 140 of the Clymer Handbook.

In short, it is important that the No. 7 lead be kept separated from the No. 8 lead, as if they get together can cause a cross fire in the engine. This generally happens when the No. 7 cylinder is firing that the No. 8 cylinder gets a H.T. voltage from the No. 7 wire and causes the No. 8 cylinder to cross fire, and this can damage the engine.

By the same token, do not allow the spark plug leads to rest on the exhaust manifolds.

The stock distributor has a very mild advance curve built into it. Most of them have the advance fully in by 2000 rpm, and the shop manual calls for only 6° advance up to a maximum of only 11°.

The Tiger will vary from engine to engine, as will any engine, but a good starting point is to set the initial advance at 9° up to 12°, if detonation isn't present and you run a good grade of premium fuel, even though the book may call for regular.

When setting the advance, remember to disconnect the vacuum pipe first before setting the initial advance. Engine idle rpm should be 6-700 for a stock warmed up engine with the choke fully open.

If a distributor test bench is available, check out the distributor curve. Point dwell settings should always be made on a distributor bench rather than by feeler gauge.

The stock Tiger's pulley is only marked up to 12 degrees advance. If you can, have the pulley fully degreed 360° or at least mark your pulley up to 40 degrees advance. It helps to make a prominent or identifying mark at the 12° and the 16° scale, as well as the Top Dead Center (T.D.C.) marker.

Once again, if you have access to a distributor bench, and in place of just checking the stock advance curve, build in a new curve that, with a fixed lead of 10°, can carry an advance of up to 36° with the distributor at full advance at 3000 rpm.

The stock factory curve:

Centrifugal Advance:

Distributor RPM	Degrees Advance
500	0-1
800	3¼-4¼
1200	5¾-7
1600	8-9½
2000	9¼-11
maximum advance limit:	11 degrees

Vacuum Advance:

Vacuum Hg"	Degrees Advance
7"	1-4
10"	5-8
14"	8-11
20"	9½-12½
maximum advance limit:	12½ degrees

Factory recommended initial advance: 6-11°

Suggested advance, initial: @ 700 rpm idle with vacuum pipe disconnected 9-12° advance.

Contact break tension: 17/20 ozs.   Dwell angle: 26/28½°

If you are willing to spend some money at this stage in place of waiting until later, then buy the dual-point distributor (Ford part No. C5ZZ-12127-D) and be done with it. This distributor if purchased separately will cost $41.50 list, or you can wait until you buy the LAT-20 camshaft kit which the distributor is part of.

This dual point distributor is a full mechanical advance unit, and the factory curve for this unit is as follows:

Distributor: 26° advance @ 7200 rpm.

Breaker gap: 018", dwell angle total: 30-33°.

Advance curve: 0 degree @ 2500 rpm and 0 in. HG Test Stand.

Distributor RPM	Degrees Advance
650	2¼ - 3¾
750	4 - 5½
1000	6½ - 7½
1600	7½ - 8¾
2000	8½ - 9¾
maximum advance limit:	14 degrees
initial advance:	12 degrees @ 7-900 rpm

The above curve is the "factory" curve, the one the distributor "should" come out of the box with. Often they don't, and the correct curve will have to be built in.

If I may, a word about building in a distributor curve. This isn't the job for the average guy in his own garage. It is a job that requires perfection. Remember to keep in mind that the distributor is the heart of your engine.

It, then, is highly recommended that only a very good distributor shop be entrusted to undertake the job of building in a new curve to a distributor.

Ideally, the best way to set up a distributor would be to have a curve plotted for the particular engine at hand. To get this type of curve, the engine is run up on a dyno at predetermined rpm ranges; the advance is made by a distributor that has no mechanical or vacuum advance mechanism but, is advanced or retarded by hand until maximum power is obtained at the given rpm. The amount of advance or retard is noted and the engine is then advanced to the next rpm range and so on up the line until the engine has covered its entire operational range. The curve thus "plotted" is then built into the distributor, matching as close as possible the curve plotted for the engine.

This would be the way to set up an all out competition engine, but too costly for the average street engine.

The next best thing, then, is to borrow a curve from an engine similar in options and features to your engine.

This also explains why the factory advance curves no longer apply when you are going to start to tune your engine for maximum power and add different than stock camshafts, carburetion, compression ratios, and even exhaust systems.

Obviously no one could sit down and say exactly how much of a curve you should carry in your own engine. For example, the carbon build-up in one engine could lower the cylinder heads combustion chamber by say 2 or even 3 c.c. This would have the effect of raising the compression of that particular engine!

So while I can recommend certain curves for distributor advances, if at all possible have your own engine plotted for the best advance curve.

With this in mind, if you have gone to the dual point distributor, the following curve will work out better than the factory curves for 90% of the Tiger engines running the stock camshaft, or the optional LAT-20 camshaft and even the LAT-1 induction kit.

Initial advance is set at 12 degrees @ 900 rpm. This is for the dual point distributor, with a fixed lead of 10° advance. Point dwell is set at a total of 34 degrees dwell.

Distributor RPM	Advance Degrees
1800	3.5
2000	4.5
3000	7.5
4000	10.0

Spark plugs used in the Tigers will be determined more by the use of the vehicle than by anything else, but a good all around plug is the Autolite BF-32 gapped at .032". This plug is to be preferred over the BF-42 recommended by the book.

When rebuilding the distributor, it is very important to keep one thing in mind. Run the unit on the bench for at least 30 minutes to make sure that the points have fully bedded in, then recheck the dwell before installing the unit in the car.

The stock Tiger carburetor is the Ford C4DF unit, a two throat downdraft unit that is just barely adequate for the Tiger. The venturi size is only 1.01" and the throttle is 1.4375" in bore size. The approximate c.f.m. flow rate is only 260 c.f.m., and thus the Tigers will actually run out of breath even before valve float sets in.

Standard main jet size for this carburetor is a 44 jet for up to 5,000 feet altitude. And since most factory carburetors have a tendency to come out of the box on the lean side, start out with a main jet of No. 46 size. The best way, of course, would be to have the car run on a chassis dyno and an air/fuel ratio check made. For maximum power a ratio of 14.8:1 should be aimed for. There are many things that prevent the ideal ratio under all conditions, so shoot for a 13.0:1 ratio at cruise and 12.8:1 under full power.

Unless you do a lot of very cold weather driving, it is a good idea for the Tiger to have its automatic choke blocked off completely. At least install a manual operated choke kit, of which there are many on the market for less than $5.00.

Outside of playing around with the jets on the stock carburetor, there isn't much you can do with it, outside of throwing it away and buying a better two-barrel such as the Holley 1-16 two-barrel. For those who really want to make the Tiger wind out on a two barrel, jump to the Holley 1-45 which has got to be the world's biggest two-barrel. Both of these carburetors will bolt right onto the Tigers stock intake manifold and all throttle linkage and gas lines will hook up. For the 1-16 model, it is a straight bolt on replacement, but for the 1-45, you'll need to enlarge the throttle holes on the intake manifold spacer about a quarter of an inch. Actually, the 1-45 would be happier with a hotter than stock camshaft anyway; so for a straight bolt on replacement carburetor for the two-barrel intake manifold use the Holley 1-16, or as an in-between step, more air flow than the 1-16, but less than the 1-45. You can always use the Holley R-2436AS, which is the center carburetor off the Ford 406 cubic inch tri-carb set up. Any one of these three Holleys will be the maximum way to go if you want to stay with a single two barrel on the stock intake manifold.

Just as food for thought, and before you start getting ideas of jumping right to a four barrel set up, let's go into the rest of the stock 260 engine and point out that it is possible to add a good 35 HP to the engine and stay with a two barrel set-up. This will really shake up your buddies with their four barrels! We'll go into this sneaky idea just a little later. Back now to the rest of the stock engine.

With the ignition and stock carburetor set up as well as you can, there isn't much else you can do except set the valves. Now don't laugh, I know this engine uses a hydraulic tappet & camshaft. You can milk the hydraulic set-up for all its worth if you set the valves like this: take the car out for a good 30 minute drive and get it really warm, none of this 5-10 idle stuff; when you get back to your garage pull one rocker cover off, and starting with the front cylinder go through each valve in the following manner. Back off the adjusting nut until lifter noise is just audible, then tighten down until it just stops, and then another quarter turn down. Proceed to the next valve and go through the entire procedure for all sixteen valves. This way you'll milk every last bit of camshaft out of the hydraulic set-up, and pick up a few rpms before floating the valves.

Remember, the useful limit of this engine/camshaft combination is going to be @ 5000 rpm tops, with power falling off sharply over 4500 rpm. A point in question on this is proven by an engine dyno test of a stock out-of-the-crate 260 Tiger engine. With everything stock output is 137 net HP at 3500 rpm; at 4500 rpm it went up to 141 HP, at 5000 rpm power fell to 135 HP and at 5500 rpm it was down to 121 HP.

There isn't any point in trying to gain additional rpm out of the stock engine for the following reasons. First the bottom end of the stock engine just isn't designed for higher rpm, and the stock connecting rods just won't take muscle over 6000 rpm. Secondly, the cylinder heads use a press-in type of rocker arm studs, and they act like a dyno; promptly at 6,000 rpm, they pull out, and thus you get a valve in the piston and that ends the whole darn test right there.

The moral is to keep everything under 5500 tops. What can be done, however, is get all the power the engine can safely handle up to the rev limits, keeping in mind at this point, we are still talking about what is basically a stock engine, with no bottom end work.

The first part of this section has been aimed at really understanding part of the HP difference between the advertised 164 gross, or 141 net, and the real power of 95-100 HP at the rear wheels.

The Tiger can be made to put out considerably more power to the rear wheels than the 100, and still keep the basic components intact. But, you'll have to do it with camshaft and carburetion.

For the maximum HP out of a two-barrel induction system, the use of the LAT-20 camshaft, and a larger two-barrel carburetor will work wonders.

At this stage of tuning the Tiger, we are going to get into the exhaust system. The stock cast-iron exhaust manifolds of the Tiger are not going to do anything for any increase in power; they will have to be replaced.

In the Sunbeam option catalog there are two sets of headers listed, the LAT-27, and the LAT-73; the LAT-27s are cast iron low loss exhaust manifolds rather than true headers, but are considerably better than the stock system.

The LAT-73 option is a true tuned length steel tube bunch of snakes, complete to the competition collectors and outlets. These are for the competition engine for developing maximum power.

The LAT-73 headers, while the most efficient set for engine operating ranges over the 4000 rpm scale, do not prove to be the best choice for engines that are operated, for the most part, under 3000 rpm.

For engines operating in the 3000 rpm range and considered street machines, the LAT-27 header system, coupled with the LAT-74, free-flow exhaust muffler system, would be considered the best choice.

The cost of the LAT-27 Header set is only $65.00, and the LAT-74 muffler system is about $52.00 for the complete set.

At this point, we are still concerned with what is considered to be a street use engine.

For the initial part of tuning the Tiger, we are considering then only the following changes: ignition, exhaust, basic carburetor. Of these initial changes, the ignition will carry over to the next step of tuning, as will the exhaust system.

The replacement of the stock Ford 2-bbl. carburetor with a Holley 2-bbl. carburetor should be considered an in between step; it will allow you to improve the breathing of the engine with a more efficient and, if you go to the Holley 1-45, a larger carburetor, yet keeping the cost down due to the fact that you are still using the original intake manifold. The use of a Holley two-throat carburetor, however, is not going to be a substitute for the LAT-1 Super induction kit, but should be thought of only as an intermediary step, allowing you to progress up to a hotter camshaft, without starving the engine.

INITIAL PERFORMANCE TUNING

It was pointed out in Section One that on a completely stock engine, you can make minor changes that will improve things all the way around. But, you can't get any great amount of power out of what you have to work with.

To start to show signs of any real increase in power, then, there are some things that are just going to have to be done no matter how you look at it.

At this point in our search for performance, we will assume that you have already gone through Section One and, (1) replaced the ignition wires with solid core wire, (2) you have added the LAT-74 exhaust system and, (3) hopefully, the LAT-27 cast iron exhaust header kit.

To start section or stage two, you will have to obtain the dual-point distributor. The engine is going to have to breathe better from this point on or forget the entire matter. And here we are going to start tearing things apart.

Since the limiting factor at this point is in the valve train, let's start there. The stock camshaft is rather mild, but nevertheless, satisfactory to do the job it was designed for. It has an absolute rpm limit of 5000 rpm.

The stock camshaft timing is as follows; @ 0 lash: Intake Opens: 21° BTC. Intake Closes: 51° ABC. Exhaust Opens: 57° BBC. Exhaust Closes: 15° ATC. Overlap is 36°, and Duration is 252°. Valve lift maximum is .380" @ 0 lash.

As was shown in Section One, the power range was from 2500 rpm up to 4500 rpm with no fall off in power.

Valve float, or rather, lifter pump-up, will set in as low as 4400 rpm's if the hydraulic tappets aren't in good shape. The single light valve springs will not allow rpm's over 5000 before floating the valves. This bump stick then is out as far as engine power is concerned.

When shopping around for a new camshaft, it's almost like being a kid in a toy shop the week before Christmas, where every toy in the world is on display, and being told to pick just ONE! Actually, trying to find a camshaft from the hundreds offered can drive a person out of his mind.

The most important thing in picking a cam is to know just what you are going to demand from the engine, as well as what the engine's limitations are in regard to the selection of a camshaft.

The Tiger has three limiting factors when it comes to choosing a camshaft. As already pointed out, the bottom end of the engine isn't strong enough for extended high rpm, the rocker arm studs will pull out at much over 6000 rpm, and the piston to valve clearance is critical in regard to camshaft or valve lift.

Taking first things first, assuming that we want to leave the bottom end of the engine alone, and that needless to say, a compression check has already pointed out the engine to be in good shape ring-wise, it would be preferable to pull the pan and check the bearings.

If everything at this point checks out, then you can start thinking about a camshaft. Let me point out at the beginning, if the engine shows any signs of weakness in the bearings and rings, it is pointless to go any further without first correcting the weak spots.

From this section on we are going to be talking about power increases of 25 and up HP, and most of it in the higher rpm ranges.

Back to the selection of the camshaft. There are many camshaft makers with all kinds of wild products on the market; some make claims of over 100 HP increase! Others have science-fiction sounding names. Still others number camshafts that sound like HP ratings.

At this time it should be pointed out that it's a lot easier to overcam an engine than to undercam one.

The Sunbeam LAT-20 camshaft kit comes complete with valve springs and tappets, the needed dual-point distributor already talked about, and an excellent all around camshaft that raises the useful rpm limit to 6000 rpm with only a slight drop in power in the low range.

This camshaft is the same camshaft that is used in the Ford 289 cu. in. Hi-Performance 271 H.P. engine, and performs very well in the 260 inch Tiger. It will, however, call for more improved carburetion to be effective.

The LAT-20 is a solid lifter camshaft that will, in a correctly set up engine, actually wind to 7000 rpm, however, power falls off much over 5600 rpm and it will take an improved valve train to go the full 7000 rpm.

For all practical purposes, then, consider the LAT-20 camshaft a 6000 rpm unit. It's most effective range is between 3500 and 5800 rpm.

The idle, or lope of this cam, is not enough to make it unsuitable for even mild street driving, and while it won't like tinkering around in tight traffic at 1500 to 2000 rpm, you can do it with a little gritting of the teeth.

This cam, when used on the stock 260 engine and the stock 260 cylinder heads, will bolt right in. You will have to remove the intake manifold, and preferably, the cylinder heads themselves to correctly install the cam and its components.

With the stock 260 heads, there will be no valve-to-piston interference, and when installing the new valve springs, if you can, install PC valve guides.

Whenever installing a new camshaft, be sure to replace the timing chain. If you can afford it at this time, replace the heavy timing gear and thick chain with the lighter gear and thin chain from a 289 Hi-Po engine. This part number is Ford No. C5OZ-6256-A (camshaft sprocket, nylon and alum.) and the timing chain is Ford part No. C3OZ-6268-A (58 links).

The LAT-20 camshaft is to be installed with no advance or retard, and as with any cam, it is always a good idea to check out the timing with a degree wheel before buttoning up the engine. They have been known to come apart, directly from the factory.

The correct timing of the LAT-20 camshaft is as follows:
@ .020" Lash; Intake Opens: 30° BTC, Intake Closes: 72° ABC, Exhaust Open: 78° BBC, Exhaust Close: 24° ATC, Overlap is 54°, Duration is 282°, Maximum lift is .457", Valve lash running clearances: Intake .018" Hot, Exhaust .020" Hot.

With this camshaft and the stock Ford 2-bbl. carburetor, the engine will put out close to 161 HP @ 5000 rpm, and will carry 150 HP @ 6000 rpm, and 141 HP @3500 rpm; it will lose about 5-7 HP over the stock camshaft below 3000 rpm however. 'Tis a sad but horrible truth that this cam will put out less power than a stocker under 3000 rpm, so, if you do all or most of your driving at 3000 rpm or under, then keep the stock hydraulic camshaft in your car!

The only other way would be to get rid of the very high 2.88:1 final drive gear that the Tiger comes with and go to a shorter gear that will allow you to keep your engine rpm up where you have some power.

To pause for a minute at this point, with the standard 2.88:1 final drive gear in the Tiger, and original equipment size tires of 5.90x13,you will have a tire height of approximately 23½". This will give you approximately 2450 rpm's at a road speed of 60 m.p.h. in fourth gear, and 2900 rpm @ 70 m.p.h. in final drive; thus with the LAT-20 camshaft, you would have to cruise at 86 m.p.h. just to get up on the cam!

Dropping the final drive gear down to a 3.76:1, however, will help things quite a bit; at 65 m.p.h. you'll be starting on the cam at 3500 rpm, and you'll still have a useful 105 m.p.h. at 5600 rpm if traffic thins out a bit; but then the 2.88:1 would give you 148 mph @ 6000 rpm. If the LAT-20 camshaft is going to be used, and it is the only optional camshaft allowed by the NHRA, if you plan on going drag racing (the LAT-20 cam, and LAT-1 induction kit engine is rated at 245 B.H.P. @ 5500 rpm), then when installing the valve springs take the extra time and install screw-in type rocker arm studs. These studs are Ford part No. C30Z-6A527-A and cost is 80¢ each; you'll need sixteen of them.

To install the new studs, simply pull out the old studs with a pair of pliers (This shows you why there is a 6000 rpm limit, doesn't it?). Tap the stud bosses for the new threaded studs, and install them only hand-tight at first. Then assemble one intake and exhaust valve on any cylinder, No. 1 preferably, and with the camshaft in the engine and tappets in place for the assembled valves, install a set of push rods. Turn the engine through by hand and check for rocker arm ratio. The correct ratio should be 1.60:1; if this is not correct, and there is trouble setting the correct valve lash, you will have to grind approximately ¼" off the stud boss and correct the rocker arm height and ratio. Do not try to correct this by shimming the push-rod height with plugs in the tappet bores. It sounds silly, but people have been known to try it that way.

Spring tension and height should also be checked very carefully, and matched to the correct height by the use of shim stock under the valve springs.

This method will prove satisfactory for the LAT-20 cam and its supplied springs, if the rpm is kept under the limit of 6000 rpms. The retainers are going to be the weak point in this system, and a set of Isky aluminum retainers should be used.

The correct spring pressure for the LAT-20 camshaft is as follows:

	intake:	exhaust:
Outer valve closed:	88 lbs. @ 1.77" /	88 lbs. @ 1.77"
Outer valve open:	247 lbs. @ 1.32" /	247 lbs. @ 1.32"
Inner valve closed:	4-7 lbs. @ 1.77" /	4-7 lbs. @ 1.77"
Inner valve open:	4-7 lbs. @ 1.32" /	4-7 lbs. @ 1.32"

This is the only factory optional camshaft in the Tiger's parts book, and is an excellent all-around camshaft if one is aware of the limitations and isn't disappointed in the poorer than stock low end performance of the car, but, wow, what it will do over that 3500 rpm hump.

Almost every cam grinder has at least a dozen or more cams for the little 260 and its big brother the 289. All will fit, and what they will do is only subject to testing. Engle has one called the No. 322 grind that is claimed to put out more HP than the LAT-20 cam, and still have enough, or rather, has a lift low enough to permit its use in the 260 with the standard flattop pistons.

I don't know if it really works, not having personally tested one and not having seen any dyno charts to judge it. However, many Mustang owners seem to like it better than the stock Hi-Po cam which is the same as the LAT-20 cam.

Another route to explore is the use of some of the newer and pretty wild hydraulic cams now available. These cams, with their anti-pump-up lifters, are claimed to be made able to go up to 7000 rpm before valve float. The only advantage I can think of in one of these cams is the valves need not be set so often, and, it's also a much quieter operation.

When it comes to picking a camshaft for the Tiger, there is a world to choose from, and the many cam grinders listed in the back of this book will send you information desired. When writing to them, explain exactly what you have done to your engine in the cylinder heads, compression ratio, bore and stroke, and induction systems, and what type exhaust you are using. Then state exactly what type of operation you have in mind for the engine. Also specify what your final drive gear ratio and tire size is, as well as the operational range you are going to use.

A very important thing to keep in mind, when selecting a camshaft for the Tiger, is the engine in stock form is fitted with flattop type pistons. These, along with the deck height of the block, account for the maximum lift you are going to be able to use.

With the use of any extremely high lift cams, you are going to have to do one of two things: fly-cut the pistons for valve clearance, or use notched type pistons such as JE or Forgetrue types with valve pockets designed in the pistons.

Engle has a cam called the 156 which works very well for an engine designed for road racing, and a line to them will get you more information on that camshaft. For drag racing, if you are allowed to use it, there is an Engle Cam known as the HL-26. It is hard to beat when the correct carburetion is used with it.

An important point on the selection of a cam, as has been pointed out, is to know just what you are going to use it for, street, drag strip, or sports car racing.

The addition of a hotter than stock camshaft in the Tiger is going to call for better carburation than the stock Ford two-barrel carburetor.

The easy way, if one is going to use the factory LAT-20 cam, wants a really hot street machine is the use of a two-barrel Holley, model 1-45 carb. This carb will have an air flow rate of 360 c.f.m., as compared to the stock 260 c.f.m. of the carburetor. It is not as expensive as a single four-barrel, costing only $30.00 or so, and will bolt right on your stock intake manifold. It will, as with the LAT-20 cam, give you a good 6000 rpm engine and not run out of breath doing it.

This combination is an excellent way to improve performance

It will be good for almost 25 HP from 3500 rpm to its limit at 6000 rpm. The combination, even with a stock 2.88:1 final drive, will give you a great third, or passing gear, just over 100 mph @ 5500 rpm! in 3rd.

Staying with the LAT-20 camshaft, use a set of 289 cu.in. 271 HP Hi-Performance cylinder heads with the big 1 7/8" intake valves, add the thin Hi-Po head gasket (yes, you can use this gasket as you will soon see), and a stock 289 engine intake manifold (the ports are a good 1/4" larger) plus the Holley 1-45 two-barrel carburetor; add to this a set of the LAT-73 headers and LAT-74 exhaust system, and you will have a really wild 260.

The fact that you are still running a single two-barrel and a cast iron intake manifold will give many of the Tiger owners with a four barrel carb a feeling of false security. There isn't any way to tell what heads you have on the block from the outside. Then kick the final drive ratio up to a 3.54:1 and you'll have the hottest two-barrel set-up you can find.

It was just said that you could use the thin head gasket of the 289 Hi-Po engine. Well, according to Ford, you can't use the 289 Gasket (thin gasket) on the 260 cylinder blocks. This is true if you have a 260 cylinder block, but most of the Tigers are coming through with what are actually 289 block only bored to 260's 3.80 bore! Thus, the 289 head gaskets will fit! How do you tell whether you have a 260 or 289 block? Simple, from the outside of the engine count the number of freeze plugs on each side; if there are three on each side, you have the 289 block, if there are only two, you have what you paid for, a 260 block, and can't use thin gaskets.

A minute for some thinking here. Say you do have the 289 block;that means you **could** bore it out to 4.00" and have yourself a 289 with the correct set of pistons. Once again, you can't bore out the 260 block to the 4.00" required on the 289.

On the subject of pistons for the Tiger, there are many types available, and with the new designs that offer "pop-top" types, you can get compression ratios all the way up to 15:1. Thus it's easy to see that the Tiger holds a great potential for power. With the initial steps to power starting to shape-up, let's explore the induction area.

Rootes offers the LAT-1, Super Induction Kit for the Tiger. This set-up, combined with the LAT-20 camshaft already discussed, will develop a rated 194 HP @ 4400. While it might not seem like any vast amount of power, it is honest HP, which is something to be considered.

Basically the LAT-1 kit consists of an aluminum intake manifold of the now popular "Hi-Riser" type. The carburetor that comes with the kit is a Holley 1-12 four barrel. The air flow rate of this carburetor is only 465 c.f.m., which is all right for street use, but isn't going to do the job for any form of competition. For competition you're going to need the Holley model R-3259-A, a huge 715 c.f.m. carburetor and it will really do the job, but the gas mileage will act like you're feeding the engine with an open hose.

The LAT-1 Induction Kit is a straight bolt-on affair. The only important thing to keep in mind, when installing the manifold, is to make sure that you follow the torque-down procedure to the letter. Aluminum manifolds are very critical, especially on the ends, and just a quick twist with a wrench will snap off the ears. It is best to use the same pattern shown in the workshop manual and follow the torque lbs/ft. as specified with the manifold.

The Tiger manifold supplied in the LAT-1 kit is made by Edelbrock Equipment Company and is the model F4B intake manifold. This is a Hi-Rise type with many counterparts. Weiand has a Hi-Riser called the Colt-65 and the Shelby-American Cobra equipment for 260/289 engines will fit too.

Surprisingly enough, the single 4-barrel set-up with the right carburetor and Hi-Riser will actually out-perform any low rise dual-quad type of system! What with the restricted space in the Tiger's engine compartment, the Hi-Rise single quad will offer few problems in mounting; but those that must have two four-barrels will find that the rear carburetor will require some alterations in the firewall to clear properly, and the linkage might present a problem.

If one wants to run a dual quad set-up, there is a unit that will really turn on: it is the new Cobra dual quad Hi-Rise outfit, but it will require a lot of metal work to fit it; so, unless you're planning a trip to the Bonneville Salt Flats, forget the dual quad set-ups.

Up to now we have three steps of power and still allowing the use of a single two-barrel carburetor and original intake manifold:
(1) Basic engine, street use, no loss of low end performance, generally improved performance, no major jump in power output.
   (a) replace the ignition radio carbon wires with solid core wiring.
   (b) rebuild the distributor with a 10° advance curve.
   (c) replace the stock exhaust system with the low loss LAT-74 muffler kit.
   (d) install LAT-5 Traction-Masters to prevent rear spring wind-up and axle hop.

(2) Basic engine, street use, slight increase in mid-range and top end power, still with 5000 rpm limit.
   (a) solid core ignition wire.
   (b) dual point distributor*.
   (c) LAT-27 header kit.
   (d) LAT-74 muffler kit.
   (e) Holley 1-16 carburetor (two barrel). The use of the Holley R-2436 AS gives slight loss of low end power.
   (f) LAT-5 Traction-Masters.

* The dual-point distributor can, as already mentioned, be purchased separately, or as part of the LAT-20 camshaft kit. From a dollars and cents point of view, it is cheaper to buy the kit than the separate parts.

For the hottest combination with a two-throat carburetor, stock cast iron intake manifold and staying with the stock bore and stroke of the basic engine, there is a combination that will wind to 6000 rpm. This combination also has a terrific mid-range and top end that will just about stay with a four-barrel set-up running a stock hydraulic camshaft. The following set-up will prove interesting; expect however, a loss of low-end power below 3500 rpm, but you'll gain almost 30 HP in the top end over a stock showroom Tiger.

   (a) Dual-point distributor and solid core ignition wires.
   (b) LAT-73 headers.
   (c) LAT-74 muffler kit.
   (d) LAT-20 camshaft kit.
   (e) Holley 1-45, two-barrel carburetor.
   (f) 289 cu. inch, 271 H.P. cylinder heads with 1.788" intake valves.
   (g) .030" thin steel head gaskets if your engine can use them. Check this.
   (h) LAT-60, H.D. Clutch assemble.
   (i) LAT-5, Traction-Masters.
   (j) LAT-50 Limited slip differential.
   (k) LAT-53, 3.54:1 final drive gear ratio.

This combination will, when correctly set up, be good for an honest 30 HP gain, just about what you would get with the LAT-1 and LAT-20 kits, without the 289 cylinder heads. For a real hot (two barrel carburetor set-up) road machine for Rally or Gymkhanas, it's the way to go.

About the only thing not mentioned on the list for this combination would be the use of the wide base aluminum wheels, part No. LAT-70 and LAT-76, heavy duty rear shocks, plus the 0-7000 rpm tach which is LAT-22.

The LAT-5 Traction Master kit on any Tiger where you are increasing the power should be considered an absolute must.

This then, is as far as one can go to really gain power out of the basically stock two barrel induction system.

Using the LAT-1 Super Induction Kit and the four barrel Holley with the Hi-Rise intake manifold is the next progressive step. It can be used either with the stock hydraulic camshaft or the LAT-20 solid lifter camshaft.

With the stock hydraulic camshaft, use the supplied Holley 1-12 of the kit, it is a small (465 c.f.m. air flow) 4-barrel carburetor, which, with the 5000 rpm limit of the stock hydraulic cam, will be very good for street and road use.

If one is going to use the LAT-1 kit with the LAT-20 camshaft, then you are going to have to use a larger carburetor such as the Holley 1-14: or for any kind of performance, you'll need the Holley R-3259 AS carburetor which is a huge 715 c.f.m. air flow unit. (This unit costs $165.00! so make sure you need it!) Actually for any except the wildest street machines, the 1-12 or the 1-14 with the LAT-20 cam would be fine.

Many Tiger owners have been tempted to buy the Ford "take-off" intake manifolds now showing up in many dealers' parts counters. Forget it! They are a cast iron low-profile four throat intake manifold, just like the ones that come on the Ford 289/225 and 271 HP engines; the carburetor is a Ford four barrel. The single two-barrel Holley No. 1-45, already mentioned, will outrun one! So, unless you can get one complete for less than $25.00, don't bother, save your money for the LAT-1 kit.

When setting up a LAT-1 or any other good Hi-Rise four barrel kit, treat the carburetor with care. The Holley is very sensitive to float level settings. (See section on carburetors.)

And do not convert the secondaries to full mechanical; leave them intact. If faster secondary openings are desired then modify the secondary vacuum unit as described in the carburetor section.

The small displacement 260 just happens to like vacuum operated secondaries, except perhaps on an all-out race car where you are always under full throttle.

There we have the basic Tiger you can get up to an honest 195 HP out of a two-barrel set-up, if you fudge a little, or you can get an honest 220 HP with no strain out of the stock engine with just using the LAT-1 and the LAT-20 kits and no fudging; take your choice. Which of the two ways to go? Admittedly to get the 195 HP out of the 2-BBL. set up requires different heads and intake manifold plus the cam and a different two-barrel carburetor; and while it has great gobs of HP in the mid-to-top end range, the stock heads, and LAT-1 and LAT-20 cam, will give you better all around performance and perhaps a few more ponies at the very top end than the big two barrel, and it will be a lot easier to gain the desired HP than the "sneaky two-barrel" set-up which requires the use of the 289 Hi-Po heads and a 289 two throat intake manifold.

Actually, the use of the 289 Hi-Po heads, while staying with the two throat carburetor and adding a hot camshaft plus tuned exhaust headers, should be really considered as a middle-of-the-road deal. Where one plans on going to the Hi-Rise four throat induction system, but is working on a part by part budget, with the eventual goal being a really super hot 260 in mind, the use of the 289 heads would be required.

The "other" route, the use of the LAT-20 cam kit and the LAT-1 induction kit, with the stock 260 heads, would be considered as the final limit or goal for a street machine.

GOING FOR TOP PERFORMANCE

From this point on, we are going after every bit of horse-power that can be pulled out of a 260 Tiger engine.

The word "rated" is mentioned many times at the beginning of this book when referring to horsepower.

Here's the way it works: when an engine is designed by a factory, a hand assembled, in fact, almost a handmade engine of the final design specifications is run to design loads under controlled conditions on engine dynos, this is without "accessories" being such things like the generator, mufflers, clutch and transmission or driveline, often without fan and mechanical fuel pump, running a very basic engine under ideal conditions.

This is where or rather how the "advertised" or rated horsepower is determined.

In the production line standards, the clearances of the engines will have a certain amount of plus or minus as for instance in the "rated" cylinder head compression ratio.

The published, or advertised, ratio of the Sunbeam Tiger's 260 cu.in. engine is 8.8:1 compression ratio. This is the maximum allowable compression ratio for the production line engine.

The acceptable range of compression ratio for a production line engine are listed as maximum and nominal. The 260 engine cylinder head combustion chamber volume in the engine specifications gives an allowance of between 53 to 56 c.c. of displacement. This, added to the distance between the top of the piston at Top Dead Center and the top of the cylinder block, an area known as deck height, plus the displacement of the cylinder head gasket itself, will give you on the Tiger a total of 66.4 to 70.2 c.c. displacement per cylinder in combustion chamber volume.

To make up for the allowable differences in production line parts then, your actual compression ratio range is from 8.4:1 up to 8.8:1.

If you had a very close machined cylinder head and minimum deck height, you would have the allowable 8.8:1 compression ratio. But on the other hand, if your cylinder head was slightly thick, in place of the minimum 53 c.c. per combustion chamber in the head, you might and probably do have 55 or 56 c.c. and instead of 8.8:1, you end up with 8.4:1. This is still within the allowable assemble line clearances, for a production line engine. It is these little things then that add up to why few engines off an asembly line will put out their rated horsepower, right out of the crate. Added to this, the required "accessories" necessary to driving the automobile therefore can cause a loss of 50% of the advertised HP to the rear wheels.

To get back some of this lost HP then is a time and money proposition. To blueprint a stock engine, that is, to rebuild the engine right to the factory specifications, means as a rule, lots of hand work and in some cases, no end of machine work. This, however, is the first step towards a racing engine.

Since many of the Tiger owners will be found at a drag strip let's explore the N.H.R.A (National Hot Rod Association) Book of Rules for building this type of racing engine first, & then go into what is known as a "Productified" S.C.C.A. or Sports Car Club of America racing engine.

The N.H.R.A. in the stock car classes, where the Tigers can run, allow nothing that isn't Sunbeam. But what you can do is "blueprint" the engine. Here we go into the world of $$$$. = HP.

To print an engine you are going to have to pull it from the car. This is also the time to go over the chassis and get rid of unwanted weight from it and the body.

The engine must be completely disassembled and every part laid out. The block and the cylinder heads should be hot-tanked. The crankshaft is going to have to be indexed and micro polished, the connecting rods full-floated, pistons replaced with hi-performance racing slugs, pin fitted and bore clearances hand honed, and block align bored and decked for height. In short, you are going to rebuild the entire engine to racing specifications for maximum power.

Taking the parts one at a time, here is what is going to have to be done to each.

Cylinder Block:

With all parts removed, hot tank the block. When completely

cleaned, including every water passage, start on the cylinder bores. The standard bore on the Tiger 260 is 3.80". Actual size limits are 3.8003/3.8027 inches. This is with no overbore. Bore spacing C/L to C/L is 4.38 inches. Setting up a Tiger 260 engine sounds extremly simple on paper. The key note, however, is careful work, overlooking no small detail.

This is why a fully printed 260 Tiger engine can cost $1,500.00 if you were to buy one outright, or you can spend $750.00 to have your own engine "printed".

The blueprinting of the basic block of the Tiger 260 engine consists of very minor work: machining of all the surfaces, deburring of the edges in the lower end, and checking and double checking of the critical areas in the crankshaft region.

Crankshaft rework consists of indexing the crankshaft, micropolishing the bearing surfaces and radiusing the oil holes in the journals.

Bearing clearances are held to within 0.0002-inch tolerances, the standard bearing clearances are .0009"-.0028". Crankshaft end play is .004"-.008". End thrust is taken by No. 3 bearing.

On the Tiger 260 engine the journal diameter and bearing overall length is as follows:

NO. 1: 2.248" x .885"
No. 2: 2.248" x .885"
No. 3: 2.248" x1.132"
No. 4: 2.248" x .885"
No. 5: 2.248" x .885"

Crankpin journal diameter: 2.123"
Direction and amount of offset: Right bank leads .84".

Connecting Rods:

The weakest point of the Tiger's engine is the stock connecting rods.

If the competition that you intend to enter allows you, replace these rods with a set of the Hi-Performance 289 cubic inch engine (271 HP version) connecting rods; this is Ford part number C30Z-6200-C, and the cost is $9.85 each. The connecting rod bolt is No. C4OZ-6214-B, the nut is No. CITE-6212-A. These connecting rods are forged steel-SAE-1041 and weigh 20.49-20.92 oz. each compared to the stock Tiger's rods that weigh only 19.97 oz. each. Overall length of both rods, stock and Hi-Po are 7.16-7.26. Length center to center is 5.155". Clearance limits for the stock 260 rods are .0011-.0027" and the end play is .010-.020". For the Hi-Po rods the clearance limits are .0015" and the end play is .014-.024".

Both engines should use plated copper-lead alloy steel back bearings, where a stock engine would use unplated copper-lead alloy steel backed bearings.

For Tiger engines that are going to see very severe service, the oil-gallery welsh-plugs at the cam-gear end of the block are replaced by screw-in plugs.

Once the crankshaft and connecting rods have been completed, as far as work is concerned, the pistons, piston pins and rings come into the picture. The stock pistons are rather heavy authothermic, aluminum alloy, tin-plated units. In stock form, they are a flat-topped configuration with steel struts, slipper skirts and cam ground.

The stock piston weight is 18.76 oz., piston only. Diameter for a stock piston is 3.7976-3.7982", and over bore sizes are available in .020", .030", .040", and .060".

The stock piston, as stated, is a flat-topped type unit without valve cut-outs; this will limit the use of very high lift camshafts, due to the valve/piston interference.

It is highly recommended that a set of hi-performance racing type pistons be used on an engine being built for any form of competition.

JE company in Monterey Park, California makes almost any type piston one could want, and since they do not make production line pistons, each set is a special order. The two types that JE specializes in for the Tiger 260 are the flat-top, and the pop-top type pistons. The flat-tops, available in any bore size, can be ordered with or without valve pockets.

The valve pockets, or fly-cuts in the JE's are large enough for the 1 $\frac{7}{8}$" intake valves. The pop-top type, or more correctly the deflector type, is a semi-wedge deflector piston which has a portion of the wedge in the intake area $\frac{1}{8}$" above the deck, or quench area of the piston.

The deflector pistons are used to gain maximum compression ratio on the Tiger 260 engine. By the use of the deflector pistons, the compression ratios can soar up to 14:1! The maximum compression ratio should not exceed 12:1 for a road-race machine with the deflector pistons using pump gasoline. A drag racing Tiger that has an all out modified engine can run as high as 14.0:1, if the engine is to be considered as an expendable type, and where the running time is measured in seconds rather than minutes or hours.

The highest compression that an engine should run, if it is to be considered a street engine, is 11.0:1, and then only when the rest of the engine has been built up to like specification. Needless to say, any compression over 10.0:1 is going to call for better than the regular grade of gasoline.

When building up an engine that is going to use the JE semi-wedge deflector type pistons to gain compression, the following items must be specified when ordering the pistons.

(1) Exact deck height from the top of a stock piston with the crank at T.D.C. to the top of the cylinder block. If the stock pistons are not available for this, then use the exact height between the top of the piston pin in the rod when the rod is in T.D.C.

(2) Exact cubic capacity of the combustion chamber.

(3) The exact measurement of the cylinder head gasket when compressed.

(4) Type of connecting rods that are to be used and material they are constructed from. (This is to compute the expansion rate of the connecting rod.)

(5) The compression ratio desired.

(6) The type of competition that the engine is being prepared for.

The JE pistons are designed, not so much on a drawing board, but are computed through an IBM machine, to meet your exact needs. Cost of the JE pistons is actually quite low, about $144.00 a set, plus $21.00 for pins and fitting.

With the crankshaft, pistons and conecting rods now in a finished state, install the bottom end of the engine. Besides using a lot of care in this department, check and double check for clearances at every move. When installing the connecting rods, slip a small piece of plastic or rubber tubing over the rod-end bolts to prevent scoring of the crankshaft.

Check for clearance between the crankshaft throws and the cylinder block, check for clearance between the piston skirts and the crankshaft throws and if necessary grind off any areas of the piston skirt that are too close. With the crankshaft, pistons and rods in place, run each piston up to Top Dead Center and check for cylinder deck height.

Mimimum deck height of the Tiger 260 is .010". In a competition engine the block will probably have to be decked to bring the deck height into minimum clearance at every cylinder. This step should not be overlooked, as your compression ratio depends on it.

Once the block and lower end components are completely brought up to specification, install the camshaft, making sure that when installing it the camshaft is coated completely with moly grease. Use care when installing the camshaft as not to nick the cam bearings. After installing the front timing gears and timing chain, bring No. 1 cylinder up to T.D.C., fill the valve pocket of No. 1 piston with modelling clay, and level with the face of the piston. Install right cylinder head with No. 1 cylinder intake and exhaust valves and rocker arm assembly. Install No. 1 cylinder push-rod and tappets.

With the head torqued down to specification, turn the engine through at least one complete revolution, stopping with No. 1

cylinder still in T.D.C. position. Remove the cylinder head and cut half the modelling clay out of the pocket with a sharp knife, checking carefully for the measurement of the valve depression in the clay.

There should be a minimum of .070" clearance between the piston and the valves, with a recommended clearance of .125". Don't hedge on the clearance since hitting a piston with a valve is no way to lighten an engine.

This method is employed when using a set of valve relined pistons such as JE's, for stock pistons where there are no cut-outs for the valves. If you are using any really hot camshaft, you are going to have to fly-cut the stock pistons.

After the pistons are checked for proper valve clearances, the engine is again torn down and all moving parts in the bottom end crankshaft, connecting rods, pistons, pins, flywheel, and clutch disc and pressure plate are to be balanced.

It is thus important to complete all machining and flycutting on the pistons before the lower end of the engine is balanced. At the same time the flywheel and clutch to be used in the unit must also be balanced.

The flywheel for the Tiger 260 in stock form is a rather heavy 20.5 pound affair, and believe it or not, the 260 engine likes it that way! The flywheel in stock trim is in an unbalanced state to compensate for the engine balance. It is a very strong unit and should be perfectly suitable for even the hardest forms of street use; however, if one is going racing, it is best to use the better material. Hays clutch and flywheel combination sets are the way to go for a race winning Tiger, and both the Hays clutch and flywheel are explosion proof and have N.H.R.A. approval. They are both highly recommended in the Tiger, having been fitted to both the Riverside Grand Prix B/Production winning Tiger and the A.H.R.A. National Record holding drag Tiger.

Cylinder Heads:

The amount of work that goes into the cylinder heads is set down by the type of competition that the Tiger is destined for. For Tigers that are to see service on the N.H.R.A. drag strips, in the stock classes the cylinder heads will receive very minor work. For the stock classes under N.H.R.A. rules, there isn't much that can be legally done outside of a good racing type valve job.

No porting or polishing is allowed under either N.H.R.A. or A.H.R.A. rules. Thus for a legal drag racing engine, all one can do is to check that the cylinder combustion chambers are correct in their allowable displacement, which on the 260 Tiger is 53/56 c.c. The engine is "rated" with a 8.8:1 compression ratio, that is, if the cylinder heads are exactly 53 c.c. To make use of the maximum compression ratio that the rules allow, the heads will probably have to be milled to get the desired 53 c.c. in each chamber. The figure 53 c.c. is the displacement in one cylinder head combustion chamber, not the total displacement for the combustion chamber with the cylinder head and gasket on the engine. The total combustion chamber volume of the 260 Tiger engine with stock bore and stroke is 66.4/70.2 c.c., with the 66.4 c.c. being the desired displacement.

To correct the cylinder to the desired displacement the following milling chart may be used, keeping in mind that when the cylinder head of the 260 Tiger is milled, the intake-manifold bottom and sides must be milled to correct the matching of the intake ports.

HEAD MILLING CHART FOR THE TIGER 260:

Heads:	Manifold Sides:	Manifold Bottom:
.010"	.012"	.017"
.020"	.025"	.034"
.030"	.037"	.052"
.040"	.049"	.069"
.050"	.062"	.086"

Milling in excess of .050" off the Tiger 260 cylinder head is not recommended. It takes approximately .0085" stock milled off the cylinder head to remove 1 c.c.

The stock 260 cylinder head gasket is of approximately .070" thickness with no compression.

Angle of valve seats in the Tiger 260 heads are 45 degrees, valve guides are integral with the heads. The valve sizes for a legal N.H.R.A. engine are as follows:
Intake Head diameter: 1.67", Length: 4.86"
Exhaust Head diameter: 1.450", Length: 4.86"

For a road racing engine you are allowed to port and polish the cylinder heads and manifolds. The correct size of the intake ports and pattern is shown in the illustration on page 30.

For road racing engines compression can be any amount. As mentioned in the section on pistons, this desired compression ratio can be gained several ways, either by the use of pop-top or semi-wedge deflector design pistons, or by very small c.c. displacement in the cylinder heads. For a figure of 11.5:1, mill the heads so that you have a 44 c.c. displacement in the chamber, and with the use of flat-top pistons you will have very close to 11.5:1.

Road racing and A.H.R.A. engines are allowed larger valve sizes. The largest listed sizes suitable for S.C.C.A. engines are 1.88" intake and 1.63" for the exhaust valves. When building up a full

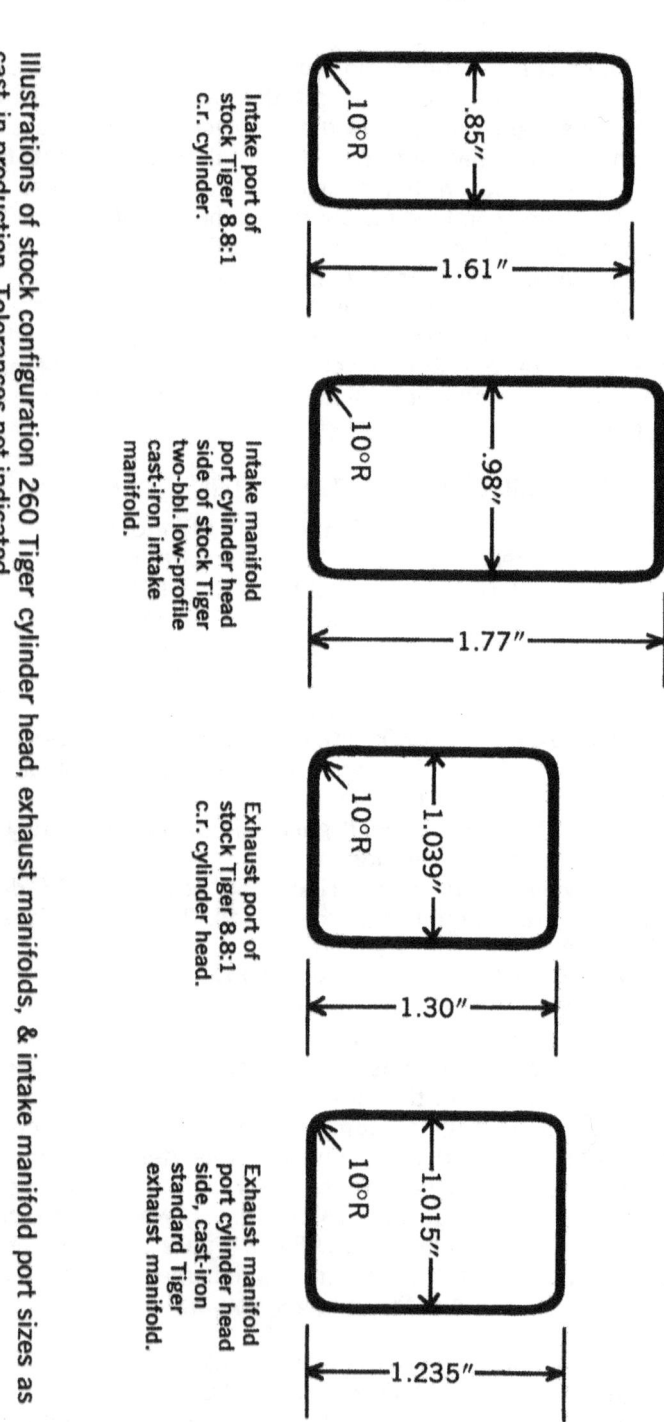

Illustrations of stock configuration 260 Tiger cylinder head, exhaust manifolds, & intake manifold port sizes as cast in production. Tolerances not indicated.

competition engine, the intake manifold should receive its share of attention; this consists of matching the manifold ports to those of the cylinder head, polishing out the passages to be certain of smooth fuel flow, connecting the primaries together and milling the manifold to reduce the gas buffeting. This work will be good for approximately 5-7 h.p.

This connecting is done to both the primary and the secondary carburetor throttle bore base as shown in illustration.

On the Tiger, when using the LAT-1 Hi-Rise intake manifold, the temperature gauge sending unit tap hole is already drilled to accept the Smith sending unit. If you are not using a Sunbeam option intake manifold, then you will have to re-drill and tap the water temperature sending unit hole to a 5/8"/18 thread pipe size. This is done if you intend to use the original Smith's water temperature dash gauge.

When installing the intake manifold, remember to torque to the letter the bolts and in their correct sequence (see torque figure section).

Before leaving the intake & cylinder head section, let's look again at the valve train and in particular the rocker arms.

The rockers on the Tiger 260 are cast units in stock form and all should be magnafluxed before being considered for serious competition use. don't be surprised if you find a 100% rejection on the set that you may have removed from your engine.

Wear factors are quite high and can be offset to some degree by having the rocker ball and contact surface of the rocker itself hard-chromed. Make sure however if you have this done that the chrome doesn't get into the inside of the rocker.

This entire method can be discarded however if you spend a few dollars and use a set of M/T (Mickey Thompson) roller rockers and special adaptors. But if you choose to do either, check your competition rules again to see if their use is allowed.

As already pointed out, on any competition engine you will have to use screw-in type rocker arm studs, and there is no shortcut on that. Once again, check your rocker arm ratio after all cylinder head, crankshaft, and camshaft work is completed.

As for the exhaust system of the Tiger, the Sunbeam option list offers the most efficient set of tuned tube-type headers you can get inside a Tiger, so use 'em.

INDUCTION SYSTEM

The stock 164 HP Tiger uses a Ford two-throat carburetor and the only other option is a Holley four-throat available in two sizes of air flow rate.

Setting up the stock Ford two barrel is a matter of following the **Sunbeam Workshop Manual** or **Clymer's Sunbeam Owners Handbook**. The Holley four-throat is another matter.

The Holley is one of the best available in a four-throat carburetor design. The standard equipment in the LAT-1 kit is a small 465 c.f.m. rated Model 1-12 Holley with the following specifications:

Throttle Bore:	Primary: 1½".	Secondary: 1½".
Venturi Diameter:	Primary: 1 3/32".	Secondary: 1 3/32".
Air flow rate:	465 c.f.m.	
Stock Jet Sizes:	Primary: 57.	Secondary: 2007-3.

This carburetor is fine for use with the standard hydraulic lifter, or stock 164 HP camshaft, but for the LAT-20 camshaft and for competition use you are going to need the larger option R-3259 AS Holley four-throat, which is as follows:

Throttle Bore:	Primary: 1 11/16".	Secondary: 1 11/16".
Venturi Diameter:	Primary: 1 5/16".	Secondary: 1 3/8".
Air flow rate:	715 c.f.m.	
Stock Jet size:	Primary: No. 67.	Secondary: No. 78.

As can be seen from the specifications, the 3259 model flows almost twice as much air as the smaller 1-12 model, and is the only one that should be considered for competition use; besides, it is the only one listed for N.H.R.A. and S.C.C.A. use.

The jet sizes of the Holley marked on the side of the jet are not the actual sizes of the openings, but rather the flow rate of the jet. This accounts for the fact that some jets when checked for size with a numbered drill will have the same apparent size of opening.

For normal use it is not advisable to re-drill the jets to a larger size. If you do decide to re-drill a set of jets, they should be marked with their new size, and not replaced in a box with unmodified jets. This method of obtaining the size of jet should really only be considered as an emergency procedure, since the actual flow characteristics of the jet are determined by not only the opening size, but length of restriction and configuration of the opening leading into the orifice of the jet.

When building up your set of jet sizes, have at least two of each size for the range you feel you will need.

You will probably find the most often used sizes are between No. 70 and No. 82.

JET SIZE FOR HOLLEY CARBURETORS

Jet Number Marked:	Closest Drill Size:
60	.055"
61	.0595
62	.0595
63	.0625
64	.0625
65	.0635
66	.0635
67	.067
68	.067
69	.070
70	.073
71	.076
72	.0785
73	.0785
74	.081
75	.082
76	.084
77	.086
78	.089
79	.091
80	.093
81	.093
82	.093
83	.094
84	.098
85	.101
86	.101

When setting up a Holley carburetor, the only really important modification is to make the secondaries operate by the original vacuum method or by means of a mechanical cam unit.

The choice is more up to the driver of the car than anyone else; however, the Tiger with its limited cubic inch displacement seems to get along better with the secondaries operating by vacuum.

There is a way of improving the vacuum operation of the secondaries so that they will open a bit faster than normal, and that is to slightly enlarge the check ball seat to increase the vacuum opening.

The Holley 3259 of the Tiger 260 is the basic Holley model 4160 design and can be used with either the standard end float bowls or the newer center-pivot float end bowls.

With the engine and carburetor reassembled in the car, the

float level must be checked again through the float level sight plugs. Before doing this the car must be set on a level surface and the engine run at idle. **Caution:** Do not attempt to adjust the float level with the engine running.

No throttle dashpot is used on the Tiger. For cars that are going to see hard acceleration use such as drag racing, the installation of small tubes inside the jets will prevent fuel from running away from the jets. This modification is not allowed in all racing rules, so check first before installing them.

The airhorn vent tubes that come in the carburetor should be replaced with longer tubes as shown in the illustration. Make certain that the tubes are pin-fitted and installed with the use of Loc-Tite, being careful that no Loc-Tite gets into the tube opening.

The importance of making certain that the tubes are not going to work loose cannot be overlooked, as they could work down into the butterflies, hang the throttles wide open, and even go into the valves.

The single 4-bbl. carburetor on the hi-rise intake manifold of the Tiger is about the best form of induction that the Tiger can handle.

Power output with the right camshaft will be equal to any dual 4-bbl. set-up on a low-rise dual quad manifold, and the only improvement would be the use of Webers or a dual quad hi-rise type system. Neither are practical due to the large amount of body work necessary to fit them under the Tiger's hood and engine compartment. In short, the LAT-1 is the way to go.

A look at a corrected bhp and corrected torque curve for the Tiger-260:

RPM:	6500	6000	5500	5000	4500	4000	3500	3000	2500	Engine Tune: see below;
BHP			121	135	141	139	137	125	108	1.
TORQ. lbs.			115	142	165	182	205	220	227	
BHP			105	131	145	141	137	127	108	2.
TORQ. lbs.			101	137	169	185	206	222	228	
BHP	129	150	160	161	159	152	141	123	101	3.
TORQ. lbs.	105	132	153	170	186	200	212	217	212	
BHP	195	204	206	197	189	173	153	124	100	4.
TORQ. lbs.	158	178	196	207	220	227	228	218	210	
BHP	211	219	222	214	201	182	158	132	105	5.
TORQ. lbs.	171	191	211	224	239	240	238	232	219	

Note: The above bhp and torque ratings are engine dyno ratings, engine running without clutch, transmission, drive line, power at the flywheel.

Engine tune from above chart:
(1) Everything stock, no changes from showroom tune specs.
(2) Reworked dual point distributor; Autolite solid core ignition wire; 9 degrees initial advance, total 36 degrees; BF-32 plugs.
(3) LAT-20 camshaft kit, Ford 2-bbl. carb. jetted w/No. 46 jets ignition as in test No. 2.
(4) LAT-1 induction kit w/Holley No. 1-12 carb., LAT-20 cam kit, ignition as in test No. 2 and 3.
(5) LAT-20 cam kit, LAT-1 induction kit w/Holley No. R-3259 carb., ignition as in test No. 2, 3, & 4, plus LAT-73 headers.

It is apparent from the above figures that power falls off past 5500 rpm with the LAT-20 cam, and past 4500 rpm with the stock hydraulic cam; yet for the most part, the hydraulic cam develops more power under 3000 rpm.

TRANSMITTING THE POWER

In the last four chapters we have concentrated on getting as much power as possible from the Tiger 260 engine. Now the time has come to concentrate on the problem of transmitting the power to the rear wheels or all previous efforts have been wasted.

CLUTCH:

The stock Tiger 164 HP clutch is a single-dry plate Ford unit of the "long" type. Stock diameter is 10 inches. The pressure plate has a total of twelve springs (6 small, 6 large). Color marking of the stock clutch springs is orange.

This unit is satisfactory for a normal road use vehicle with the stock 164 engine. It is not going to do the job for really hot road engines, and certainly will not be suitable for any form of competition use.

The only Sunbeam option is the LAT-60 heavy duty clutch. This unit will be suitable for the hottest street machines and rally use cars. It still is not going to do the job on a racing or competition machine.

To examine what we have to work with in the Tiger-260 as far as clutches are concerned, here are the specifications of the two Sunbeam units:

Stock, 164 hp. original equipment clutch
Type: Semi-centrifugal single dry plate disc.
Type pressure plate springs: Coil
No. and color marking: 12, orange
Effective plate pressure, lbs.: 1260
Material of clutch facing: Woven asbestos
Outside and inside dia.: 10.0 x 6.75 inches
Total effective area: 86.2 sq. in.

Thickness: 125"
Engagement cushioning method: Torbend disc.
Release bearing, type: Ball thrust, prepack, sealed.
Torsional damping: Springs.
Sunbeam Option LAT-60 Heavy Duty Clutch
Effective plate pressure, lbs.: 1611
Everything else the same as the stock clutch except outside diameter, which on the H.D. LAT-60 is 10.5".

From this it is easy to see why the optional H.D. clutch is only of use for the hotter road machines, and not for competition cars.

Both the standard and the H.D. clutches are fully counter-weighted type pressure plate units. This type of clutch isn't going to be useful in competition. The counter-weights are designed to add additional pressure to the pressure plate under higher rpm's by the same token, make the clutch almost impossible to shift fast at those same high rpm.

For competition-use Tigers it is highly recommended that a Hays clutch, disc and flywheel assembly be used.

The Hays clutch units are explosion proof, and are supplied without counter-weights. They are designed for and work extremely well in the Tigers.

Since the Tigers use a hydraulic slave cylinder, it isn't advisable to exceed 24-2600 lbs. pressure on the pressure plate.

Many racing organizations now forbid the use of stock flywheels, so it is a good idea to use the new Hays Steel Billet flywheel, which is also explosion proof and is slightly heavier than the stock unit.

The Hays clutch and disc unit used in the Tiger is the Invader series. (Hays' address can be found in the back of the book).

When installing a new clutch always use a new throw-out bearing, and be sure to always inspect the clutch release arm to make certain that it isn't bent. Always inspect the slave and master cylinders before completing the job.

Pay particular attention to the hydraulic pipe connecting the master cylinder to the slave cylinder. This pipe is quite brittle, and hairline cracks can develop in it allowing the loss of hydraulic fluid.

When installing the hydraulic pipe, use a bit of Teflon instrument tape over the threads to ensure a good work-free fit in the cylinders.

Inspect the flared ends of the pipe fittings and polish the tapered flares to ensure a snug fit.

Caution: the Tiger should only be filled with Girling amber fluid, in both the clutch and brake master cylinders.

After installation of the clutch, be sure that you bleed the system, since the Tiger's slave unit offers no adjustment. This is very important.

There are many racing type clutches on the market, some good, some not so good. Be certain when you order one that you get one from a manufacturer that has a perfect reputation.

The companies listed in the back of this book all make excellent racing clutches. However, the author's personal recommendation is the Hays clutch, disc and flywheel combination.

It should well be pointed out that no rebuilt clutch unit should ever be considered for any type of competition or racing machine.

The use of a scatter-shield, such as the Sunbeam optional LAT-7 (Steel wedge bell-housing), should be considered a must and is required in many racing rules. This option is N.H.R.A. and A.H.R.A. approved for use, and even with the best made racing clutch/flywheel assembly, it is a wise investment. Remember, you only have two legs, and a blown clutch or flywheel can also make a mess out on the track.

The transmission that is standard on the Tigers with serial numbers from B-9470057 on up to the latest all use the Ford heavy duty transmission, either the HEH-E, or the HEH-B units, with the following ratios:

HEH-E	HEH-B
1st: 2.32:1	1st: 2.78:1
2nd: 1.69:1	2nd: 1.93:1
3rd: 1.29:1	3rd: 1.36:1
4th: 1.00:1	4th: 1.00:1
Rev: 2.32:1	Rev: 2.78:1

The type used on your car will be marked on the transmission case, which is the "top-cover" type. The HEH-E is the preferred set of ratios for competition use.

Some of the first Tigers, with serial numbers below 9470057, were fitted with the very popular and desirable Warner T-10 transmission, featuring the 2.20:1 low and close ratios. These were available in both the steel case and the lightweight aluminum case, which was more suitable for racing. It is, however, no longer available, except under special order as long as the limited supply lasts. For the lucky '65 Tigers that have it, the ratios are as follows:

1st: 2.20:1
2nd: 1.62:1
3rd: 1.20:1
4th: 1.00:1
Rev: 2.20:1

The third member, or final drive of the Tiger, is the healthy Salisbury hypoid 4.HA unit. It is strong enough to hold two Tigers. In stock trim, the final drive ratio without a limited slip differential is a high 2.88:1. This ratio, while fine for good gas mileage, or terrific top ends, isn't going to do anything at the traffic lights except bog.

Sunbeam has a complete set of gear ratios in an excellent limited slip unit that range from a high of 3.07:1 to a low of 3.73:1.

This range is going to be satisfactory for almost any street, rally or road racing use, but for a Tiger that is going to the drag strip you are going to need a very low 4.55:1 gear.

To get this gear you will need to visit two non-Sunbeam dealers. First, go to a Studebaker dealer and order a 1961 Commander ring-gear and pinion set number 531156, which is the 4.55:1 assembly. Next go to a Kaiser-Willys dealer and order the Jeep Wagoneer limited-slip differential part number 935638. This is for a J-series Power-Loc and a 44-1 axle.

The combination of the Studebaker ring-gear and pinion and the Jeep limited slip differential will give you the needed 4.55:1 gearing. Both units will fit right in the original third member case, but remember that you will have to use the Rootes tool gear carrier stretching fixture No. SL.1A or Kent-Moore J5231-01. It is best to leave the changing of the rear axle gears to a Sunbeam dealer's service department.

CHASSIS TUNING

The Tiger in stock trim understeers, and even in competition trim it is still going to understeer. The object, then, is to make the handling as nearly neutral as possible.

The stock shock absorbers are alright for about 2,000 miles street use, then they've had it.

Since you're going to have to replace the shocks then any way, you have several choices, the popular Konis, or the Sunbeam optional LAT-76 and LAT-77 hi-performance shocks.

These are a very good replacement for a high-speed road or rally car, but for a competition car you will have to go to the Konis front and rear. The only optional rear setup would be to use the S.C.C.A. approved lever shocks. For information on this you'll have to write to International Automobiles Inc., Sunbeam Tiger Division, Los Angeles (See rear of book for address).

Sunbeam has available several different sizes of front roll bars and springs in various setting rates, so that for a road racing Tiger one can modify the suspension to one's own preference. The rear suspension is going to need some help to prevent the rear axle from hopping and getting spring windup under heavy acceleration and braking loads.

This problem can be solved by the use of the LAT-5 Traction-Masters and the LAT-76/77 HD shock absorber kits, and is not only recommended for competition models, but for all Tigers in general.

The handling can be further improved by the use of wider base wheels, such as the LAT-70 aluminum option wheels. These are 5.50 x 13" wheels and will gain you a full inch (4½" x 13" stock) over the original equipment.

Tire choice is a matter of use and personal preference more than anything else. About all that can be recommended in the tire department is that you use a top quality high-speed rated tire of the largest size you can get under the fender wells. On an unmodified Tiger, this will be your limiting factor.

Firestone 500 6.50 x 13 tires are a good choice and are a 125 mph rated tire for road use. This is not a racing tire, however, but a good road and rally tire.

Goodyear has the Power-Cushion in the Tiger's sizes, and both Goodyear and Firestone in 1967 have the new Wide-Oval type tires. It is hoped that these will be available in 13" sizes to fit the Tiger, which needs a big footprint of rubber on the ground, even in street trim.

The radial type tires are available from every tire company making them in 13 inch sizes, and the size to fit the Tiger is a 165 x 13. If your Tiger has a slightly larger front splash opening you can fit the 175 x 13 radials, but check for clearance with the front wheels at full lock in both directions. You may need to do some metal cutting for the larger tires.

There are two limiting factors in the rear tire sizes. Clearance between the fender lip on the outside, and clearance between the springs on the inside. There should be maximum clearance for both since on a hard turn you could cut a tire apart by rubbing on the springs or the fender lip.

The tire pressures recommended by the tire manufacturers should be followed, and the front and rear alignment should be checked as described in the workshop manual.

THE CUSTOM TIGER

Up to this point most of the improved performance in the Tiger's engine department has been gained through the use of

Sunbeam options, and there's nothing wrong with being able to jump your stock HP from a net of 141 BHP @ 4400 rpm to over 200 BHP @ 5500 rpm and do this with only minor factory options.

The Tiger, however, being blessed with one of the most popular engines to come on the postwar scene since the 265 cubic inch Chevy V-8, has gained the notice of many speed and custom equipment manufacturers in the U.S.

What this means to a Tiger owner is that a gold mine of performance and styling options are available to choose from.

Starting with the subject of wheels, besides the Sunbeam option LAT-70, which is a 5.5 x 13" cast aluminum wheel, there is a set of competition wheels available from American Racing Equipment. These come in widths up to 6 x 13" from stock, with different degrees of offset.

The important thing to remember when shopping for wheels for the Tiger is to be sure to try a set on your car to check for clearance between fender, and in the rear, spring clearances.

Due to the odd bolt pattern of the Tiger's wheel and offset required, your selection of wheels is going to be somewhat limited.

Grill guards are available from many accessory shops such as MG Mitten and Vilem B. Haan.

Fog lights, driving lights, luggage and ski racks are part of the available dress-up items that can be found in parts houses.

For Tiger owners who leave their cars outside with no garage, an MG-Mitten cover is a very good investment.

The Tiger uses a very attractive wood finish 15½" steering wheel. You're going to have to live with it, as the Tiger's adjustable steering wheel boss also contains the electrical fittings for the horn, turn indicators, and headlight flasher. There isn't, to my knowledge, an accessory wheel that will fit the Tiger.

Radios are available that range from the manual tuning AM models up to push-button AM/FM models, and your taste and budget can decide which you want.

The Tigers come with a rather complete set of standard instruments, the only options being the Sunbeam electric clock and ammeter.

Dressing up the engine compartment is a very simple thing to do. The Sunbeam option list includes a set of polished and finned aluminum valve covers, a chrome air-cleaner cover and oil filler cap.

Almost every speed and custom equipment maker also has a line of aluminum valve covers in various designs. The one thing to keep in mind when shopping for cast aluminum valve covers for the Tiger is to make sure that they clear under the firewall;

some will not, due to their additional height. The set in the Sunbeam options has the rear part of the valve cover lowered to clear the firewall panel.

The standard Tiger's tach reads up to 5000 rpm, and there is an optional tach that reads up to 7000 rpm, a straight fit replacement.

Other tachs can be used in the Tiger, but it is often necessary to use an adaptor plate in the dash mounting hole.

The Tiger owner need not rely just on the Sunbeam option kits. There are many other power adding kits available from other suppliers that give a wide choice of tuning stages.

Weiand makes a very good single quad Hi-Rise intake manifold, a dual quad manifold and a cross-ram intake manifold. Camshafts for the Tiger are available from Potvin in five different grinds and roller tappet grinds ranging from 284 to 335°. These start at prices around $320.00 for the complete kit.

Racer Brown has a new Revmaster 101-M, which it is claimed will outperform the LAT-20 cam and still be usable in street machines. Racer Brown also makes a 7000 rpm hydraulic cam, the Revmaster 202-H.

Crane Cams have a very good reputation with the builders of the hottest 260/289 engines. They have a road and drag cam for hot street engines called the H-260 Hydraulic, which puts out slightly more power than the LAT-20, yet offers the ease of maintenance of the hydraulic tappets. The cost is $177.00 for the complete kit with tappets. For maximum performance engines, the Crane Ramsonic Hyper Flo Roller has a valve lift of 0.587" and sells for $342.00. Engle camshafts enjoy an excellent reputation on the West Coast. They make a No. 322 cam and kit which is supposed to be the hottest thing that you can use in the Tiger with standard flat top pistons. Engle claim 35 additional HP over the LAT-20 camshaft kit from their cam.

A new name in the camshaft field for Tiger owners is Dempsey Wilson. Dempsey has in the last year or so come up with some really swinging camshafts for the 260 Tiger engine and as with the old faithful Iskenderian, has so many cams that he can't count them. It would be wise to write to several manufacturers and state exactly what you need in the way of power, what you are going to do to your engine, and listen to their advice.

It was mentioned earlier that when you pick a camshaft for the Tiger and plan to use the stock flat topped pistons, the valve-to-piston clearance is a limiting factor. The following rule of thumb should be used in picking a camshaft for the Tiger 260:

Maximum lift: .440" Maximum overlap: 56°

The LAT-20 Sunbeam cam exceeds the lift, but not the overlap. Therefore it is usable in the Tiger with flat topped pistons, provided that you are using the stock cylinder heads with original 1.67" intake valves.

If you are running large valves, then even with the LAT-20 cam you will probably have to notch the pistons for valve clearance.

TUNING TO WIN

When a Tiger is to be set up for specific competition purposes it should no longer be considered as an all-around vehicle, but a machine that is designed and built to do one basic thing: win! There are no short cuts to making a winning machine.

The three most popular competitive events in the U.S., as far as sports car owners are concerned, are road racing S.C.C.A. style, drag-racing N.H.R.A. and A.H.R.A style, and Slalom events. Let's explore what it is going to take to set up a Tiger specifically for the events at hand with one idea in mind, to win.

The S.C.C.A. events place the Tiger in the Class B, Production Sports Cars category. In this you are allowed quite a few changes in the car and still be considered "production."

For a car to be set up to the legal limit of the rules is the final goal. To fail to take advantage of every single rule and loophole is to end up in second place.

Starting with a showroom stock Tiger, to go road racing you first pull the engine, transmission, and rear axle out of the car.

The engine is then completely torn apart and rebuilt to racing specifications as described in the section on "blueprinting". The transmission is taken apart, gears hand-lapped, and ratios changed to suit the driver and circuit.

When building up an engine for S.C.C.A. club events, get a copy of the **S.C.C.A. Production Car Classes**, and the **S.C.C.A. Car Classification Guide**. In the section dealing with the Sunbeam Tiger, you'll find what "options" are allowed by the rules. For 1966, a quick look showed that you were allowed up to the following limits on valve sizes. Intake: 1.88" maximum, compared to the stock 1.67" valves. Exhaust: 1.63" compared to the stock 1.45" valves.

Under S.C.C.A. rules, you are allowed to run any cylinder head compression. Your stock compression ratio, remember, is only 8.8:1 tops; kick this up for S.C.C.A. races to 11.25:1.

Use a camshaft reground to Engle No. 156 specification. Note I say "use a reground' cam, for the rules say you must use "any reground original cam". Take a brand new stock LAT-20 camshaft to Engle and have them regrind it to No. 156 specifications.

Use the LAT-1 kit, add the optional R-3259 AS Holley carburetor. Start out with jet sizes of No. 76 in the primaries, No. 79 in the secondaries. Take advantage of the allowable overbore and bore to the limit of the permitted .040" overbore. Your stroke, however, must remain a stock 2.87".

In the gearbox ratios, for 1966, you have a choice of the following ratios:

	Set A	Set B	Set C	Set D
1st:	2.32:1	2.20:1	2.20:1	2.36:1
2nd:	1.69:1	1.63:1	1.48:1	1.63:1
3rd:	1.29:1	1.31:1	1.18:1	1.21:1
4th:	1.00:1	1.00:1	1.00:1	1.00:1

The choice of set, will be dictated by the course, as will final drive gears.

In their S.C.C.A. approved option list Sunbeam has a very lightweight rear end and limited-slip unit. It is a 33-1 series axle setup. While it does reduce the unsprung weight, it is very delicate and subject to breaking under any kind of hard racing start. It is recommended that you stay with the heavier 44-1 axle or standard LAT-50 limited-slip unit and its available gears.

For racing use get a set of HD brake pads, Ferodo or Grey Rock and use metallic rear linings.

Always use Girling amber fluid in both the clutch and brake cylinders. As far as the suspension goes, no one can say just what someone else will want in the handling of a car, so this you'll be better off working out for yourself. You will, however, find that the Konis up front will work out very well as far as shocks go. Sunbeam has listed a set of lever type rear shocks for competition that have 22 different adjustments! You should find one that works for you in that department.

You want the widest wheel you can get under the Tiger so use the American Racing Mag, either 5.5x13 or 6x13" sizes. You will have to flare out the fenders to use them. For tires in road racing you might try a set of the Firestone Super Sport Indy in the 5.50 x 9.50 x 13" size; this tire has the following specifications:

Tire: 5.50 x 9.50 x 13"
Height: 23.46"
Tread: 7.67"
Cross section: 9.83"

The compound of the "Indy" is a 104, its list price is $35.95 plus tax. It is, by the way, a good slalom tire.

The body for road racing has to undergo a drastic diet. All the undercoating, interior jute, carpeting, floor mats, have to go.

You'll need to remove the windscreen and make a plexiglass racing screen. The door windows come off, as will the folding top. The heater and defroster will end up in the useless spare parts bin, and a roll bar is going to have to be built and competition seat belts fitted. Mount a fire extinguisher where the driver can get to it quickly yet where it won't interfere with his driving actions.

The bumpers must come off and you are going to have to fit an oil cooler, and cut cooling outlets in the fenders and hood. The hood should be set up with an airscoop and quick release pins to prevent the hood from flying off.

As far as the engine accessories are concerned, replace the generator pulley with a deep-dish type and use either a Gates racing or Atlas fan belt.

Double solder the radiator tubes that connect the water expansion or header tank. These are small brass tubes, one on the radiator, one on the header tank are very weak and will fracture every time you remove the small connecting hose. It's a good idea to cross brace these tubes.

This isn't going to tell you step-by-step how to build a race car, but it will show you what you're going to have to do as a starting point.

Going next to the drag-racing Tigers, here is an area where Tiger owners can have a field day, for it is one of the biggest sleepers to ever hit this form of racing.

To set up a Tiger for the drags you must first decide which group of drag racing you want to run, the N.H.R.A. (National Hot Rod Association) or the A.H.R.A. (American Hot Rod Association).

Their rules are different. The N.H.R.A., the largest of the two organizations, places the Tiger in two classes for 1967. For the "Stock" 164 BHP rated engines, running the single two-barrel carburetor and factory hydraulic tappet camshaft, the Tiger will run in the following classes:

Engine: 164 bhp

Roadster, shipping wt.: 2,520 lbs. min.
    15.39 lbs. per hp., 1967 N.H.R.A. Class: H/S

GT Tiger (hard-top, factory top) shipping wt.: 2,574 lbs.
    15.69 lbs. per hp., 1967 N.H.R.A. Class I/S

Engine: 245 bhp, single 4/bbl. Holley No. 3259 carb. Hi-rise manifold, solid lifter camshaft LAT-20.

Roadster and GT:
10.28 lbs. per hp (roadster): B/S
10.50 lbs. per hp (GT): B/S

The N.H.R.A. events use as a system of power to weight scale for car classification in the "Stock Car Classes". To determine the class that you car will run, you divide the vehicle's advertised shipping weight by the factory-advertised horsepower. So many pounds per HP will give you the class breakdown.

Before entering the N.H.R.A. events you should buy a copy of the latest issue of the N.H.R.A. official drag rules. Copies are available from the N.H.R.A. office at 3418 First Street, Los Angeles, California 90004.

For Tigers wanting to run "Stock Class," as was already pointed out, you will not be allowed to run with all the sports car racing options listed in the S.C.C.A. rule books. You will only be allowed to run one of two models of the Tiger, the 164 BHP engine version with the stock Ford 2-bbl. carb and the hydraulic stock camshaft, or the 245 HP version with the LAT-1, & LAT-20 kits. You are only allowed to run a maximum of 8.8:1 compression ratio and no porting or polishing is allowed.

You are allowed only a .030" overbore in the NHRA, but you can run the LAT-73 headers and any gear ratio that will fit in the original third member case. You are allowed to use the LAT-70 aluminum wheels and you can run any size tire not smaller than the original equipment size. You must run the full windscreen and all interior upholstery. For a drag racing Tiger you can't gut or strip the car, or remove the bumpers.

In short, a drag racing Tiger must be almost in showroom condition. You are not allowed to run the fiberglass optional hood with airscoops or cooling vents, at least not until the factory makes 500 of them.

For drag racing you'll want to use the standard original equipment shock absorbers in the rear, the LAT-5 Traction-Masters, and the LAT-77 front shocks.

You should consider the Hays clutch and flywheel a must for drag racing use, and the LAT-7 scatter-shield will be required.

An oil cooler is allowed and should be fitted. Also use the HEH-E transmission gears, the LAT-50 limited slip and the lowest (high numbered) gears you can pull. The use of the factory hard-top, No. 2220740 will give you a class advantage in weight.

For drag racing in the A.H.R.A. events, you are allowed much more freedom in modifying the car. You can run any flat-tappet camshaft, any carburetor that will fit on the original intake or optional intake manifold, any cylinder head and valve size and any compression ratio. However, you still cannot port and polish the cylinder heads.

The A.H.R.A. has classes for the foreign sports cars, where the N.H.R.A. will run the Tigers in the regular stock car classes.

Given a choice, set up your car for the N.H.R.A., and then you can run either event. If you set up the Tiger for A.H.R.A., you'll have to run Modified Sports in the N.H.R.A., which is a school left open to your own skill. (You had better be prepared to run in the low 11 second range).

The Slalom events are fast becoming popular on the West Coast as they have been on the East Coast for some time, and setting up a Tiger for Slalom events will give you plenty of room to play around with your own ideas.

You can run any type of carburetor that will fit on the original or optional intake manifold, as well as any tires and wheels, cam, heads, and port and polish to your heart's content.

In short, you can set up your car for road racing with almost no restrictions as to what you can do in the suspension or engine departments short of switching the engine to a 426 Hemi and claiming "just a slight overbore".

SUPPLIERS DIRECTORY

CAMSHAFTS AND VALVE TRAIN:
Engle Racing Cams,
1621 Twelfth Street,
Santa Monica, California 90404
Phone: 213/ 451-1476

Dempsey Wilson Racing Camshafts,
4667 W. Rosecrans
Hawthorne, California
Phone: 213/ 675-5558

Crane Engineering Co.,
100 N.W. 9th Terrace,
P.O. Box 160, Hallandale, Florida
Phone: 305/ 927-4261

Potvin Equipment Co.,
111 E. Wilhelmina,
Anaheim, Calif.

Racer Brown Inc.,
108 W. Florence Ave.,
Inglewood, Calif.

Crower Cams & Equipment Co.,
3333 Main Street,
Chula Vista, California 92011
Phone: 714/422-1178

Howards Power and Racing Equipment,
10122 S. Main St.,
Los Angeles, Calif.

Chet Herbert Cams,
1933 Manchester,
Anaheim, California
Phone: 714/ JE 7-1246

Weber Speed Equipment,
310 S. Center Street
Santa Ana, California 92703
Phone: 714/ 547-2595

Ed Iskenderian Racing Cams,
16020 S. Broadway,
Gardena, California 90247
Phone: 213/ 770-0930

CLUTCHES AND FLYWHEELS:
Hays Clutches and Flywheels,
15118 Adams Street,
Midway City, California,
Phone: 714/ 892-3957

Schiefer Mfg. Co.,
508 Monterey Pass Road,
Monterey Park, Calif.

Weber Speed Equip.,
see address under camshaft listings.

PISTONS:
JE Engineering Corp.,
930 Monterey Pass Road,
Monterey Park, Calif.

Jahns Quality Pistons, Inc.,
2662 Lacy St.,
Los Angeles, Calif.

INDUCTION MANIFOLDS:
Weiand Power And Racing Equipment,
2737 San Fernando Road,
Los Angeles, California 90065

Offenhauser Sales Corp.,
5300 Alhambra Ave.,
Los Angeles, Calif.

Edelbrock Equipment,
4921 W. Jefferson Blvd.,
Los Angeles, California

Shelby-American, Inc.,
6501 W. Imperial Highway,
Los Angeles, Calif.

RACING TIRES:
Firestone Tire and Rubber Co.,
1200 Firestone Parkway,
Akron, Ohio 44317

Goodyear Tire and Rubber Co.,
Akron Ohio, 44317

Dunlop Tire and Rubber Corp.,
P.O. Box 2011,
Buffalo, N.Y.

Michelin Tire Corp.,
P.O. Box 217,
Woodside, 77, N.Y.

SUNBEAM FACTORY COMPETITION OPTIONS:
International Automobiles, Inc.,
9830 West Pico Blvd.,
Los Angeles, California, 90035
Sunbeam Tiger Division
c/o Mr. R. G. Wheatly 213/ 276-4161

DRESS-UP ITEMS:
MG Mitten, Inc.,
1163 E. Green Street
Pasadena, California

Vilem B. Haan, Inc.,
10305-07 Santa Monica Blvd.,
W. Los Angeles, California 90025

Bell Auto Parts,
3663 E. Gage Ave.,
Bell, California

Products d'Elegance
3639 San Fernando Rd.,
Glendale, California

All of the listed companies will send information on specific products, and most have catalogs available at slight charge. When writing, state your requirements fully so that they can be of complete help in your selection.

INSTALLATION TIPS — LAT OPTIONS

When installing the LAT- options, it should be pointed out that to correctly set up a Tiger 260 engine it should be removed from the chassis. This is due to the limited working room around the engine in the body.

It is possible however to install the LAT-1, induction kits and the LAT-20 camshaft kits without removing the complete engine. This should be done only if the budget and equipment is not available to correctly remove the engine.

For the installation of the LAT-1 induction kit, it is a simple matter of following the normal procedures of removing the old intake manifold, as described in the workshop manual.

The LAT-1 kits come with a fair set of instructions for installation of the Hi-Rise kit.

The following procedures will be helpful in updating the instructions that come with the LAT-1 kit:

LAT-1 Kit:

(1) Remove radiator shroud, radiator and hoses from engine. This is not a requirement, but will help in the correct installation of the kit.
(2) Remove the valve covers from both sides and the smog-device from the carburetor base spacer plate.
(3) Remove the heater (if fitted) water hoses and the water temp sending unit.
(4) Remove the distributor, first making sure that the engine is on No. 1 TDC.
(5) Remove all intake manifold bolts and save. Remove the intake manifold with thermostat water housing attached.
(6) If at this time you are only going to install the LAT-1 kit and no camshaft kit, open the kit, lay out all parts, check

against the enclosed instructions and make certain that you have a complete set of fittings, gaskets, and new bolts where required.
(7) Scrape away all old gaskets from the cylinder heads and front and end cover gaskets.
(8) Do **not** at this time install new carburetor.
(9) Install new gaskets as you would for stock intake manifold as per workshop manual.
(10) Install old water thermostat housing from old manifold to new manifold after first inspecting for condition. The housing is part number C30Z-8594-B (water top, outlet-pipe) and the gasket is part number C30Z-8255-A. This housing is only pot-metal, and is cheap enough to replace if any signs of deterioration are present. **Note:** when installing this new housing and gasket along with the correct thermostat (160°, part No. C-2UZ-8575-B) do not over-tighten, as they will easily break.
(11) Install the temperature sending unit in new manifold.
(12) Install elbow fitting for brake servo vacuum fitting.
(13) With intake manifold gaskets in place carefully install new manifold, making sure that you do **not** shift the positions of the gaskets.
(14) With the new manifold in place, start the manifold tightening sequence as shown in the illustration. Correct torque is 15 lbs. ft.
Start with all bolts torqued down to approximately 8 lbs.; then repeating the correct sequence, bring down to 12 lbs. and finally down to 15 lbs. for the aluminum intake manifolds.

Before installing new carburetor see footnote*

(15) Install new carburetor gasket, spacer plate and new carburetor. Connect the brake and smog-device hoses. The water hose to the heater will no longer run under the carburetor through a spacer plate.
(16) Install the radiator, and connect all water hoses.
(17) Following instructions in LAT-1 kit, install fuel lines and distributor.
(18) Refill the radiator with water with car heater controls set to "hot", and bleed the water lines to make certain that any trapped air is removed. Check for any water leaks.
(19) Attach the original carburetor linkage to the new carburetor, check for full throttle opening and adjust the linkage as described in workshop manual if necessary.
(20) When installing the LAT-1 kit, replace the fuel filter if pos-

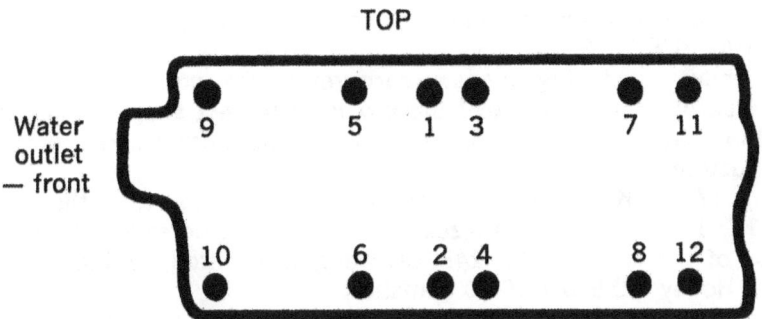

Intake Manifold Torquing Sequence
Maximum Torque 15 foot lbs.

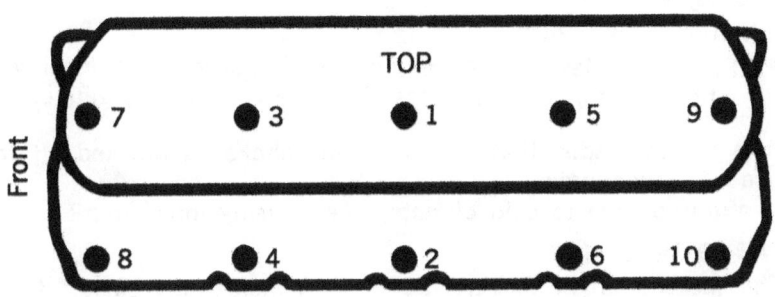

Cylinder Head Torquing Sequence
Maximum Torque 68 foot lbs.

sible at this time. Also replace the air filter before installing air-cleaner cover.
(21) Before starting engine and after completing the LAT-1 installation, turn on ignition key. Without starting engine, check for fuel leaks in carburetor and fuel lines.
(22) After completed installation, set carburetion idle and recheck ignition timing after complete engine warm-up.

* CARBURETOR NOTES

Whenever installing a new carburetor, **Do not assume that the carburetor right out of the box is in perfect shape.** It is possible that in the shipping the float levels were shaken out of adjustment.

The LAT-1 Kit uses a Holley 4-bbl. carburetor in either the 1-12, 1-14 or the 3259 sizes, the sizes being determined by the use of the vehicle. The 245 BHP engine is fitted originally with the Holley 3259 & LAT-20 camshaft.

The LAT-1 kit, if purchased separately, is supplied with the model 1-12 carburetor, which is more suited for the 164 HP engine stock camshaft.

All the Holleys are of the 4160 type, and the following basic specifications will apply.

Holley 4160

Idle Adjustments:

Idle fuel screw: 1 turn.

Fast idle: Float level — Wet: engine running at idle; just level with bottom of inspection holes. Dry: use Ford/Holley gauge.

It is recommended that the automatic choke be blocked off for use with Tiger engines.
If required due to cold climate, use housing index mark.

LAT-20 Camshaft Kit:

The installation of the LAT-20 kit is considerably easier if the engine is removed from the chassis. If this is not practical the LAT-20 kit can be installed using the following technique.
(1) Remove the complete intake manifold.
(2) Remove the radiator and all water hoses.
(3) Remove the front section of the engine, water pump, fan, crankshaft pulley and front cover assembly.
(4) Remove the exhaust manifolds.
(5) Remove the cylinder heads.
(6) Remove the grill bar badge from the center. When the engine is torn down remove the old hydraulic tappets, clean off old gasket material.

The new camshaft is installed in the same manner as is a stock cam following the workshop manual. Remember to coat the new camshaft with a moly type grease before installation.

(7) Install the new lifters, also coating with moly grease.
(8) Replace the valve springs with the new camshaft kit valve springs after first checking their height and pressure as per specifications in earlier part of book.
(9) Install new valve guide seals and if possible PC seals.
(10) After installation of new valve springs in the cylinder heads, check all rocker arms for any wear or cracks, and replace any required.
(11) When the camshaft is installed in the engine, replace the timing chain and gears. You should use a new timing chain and gears.
(12) Install No. 4 and 8 cylinder pushrods **before installing the cylinder heads!**
(13) Install the cylinder heads, pushrods, and reassemble engine.
(14) Set valve clearance to .022" intake and exhaust when cold. Warm up engine for at least 30 minutes before setting final valve clearance which is .018" intake hot and running, and .020" for the exhaust hot and running.

TROUBLESHOOTING

The Sunbeam Tiger 260 is one of the most trouble-free sports cars on the market today. Owners report very few major problems with the exception, perhaps, of the carburetor or fuel system, and a fault which has bothered many Tiger owners, heating!

Taking the two most common problems, fuel system and heating let's explore the main symptoms.

The Tiger uses a full pressure cooling system with a crossflow radiator and water expansion or header tank. A vane-type, cast iron impeller supplies coolant through centrifugal action to the water pump outlet ports, one for each cylinder bank, to provide uniform coolant circulation in both banks of the engine.

The water pump has a sealed bearing which is integral with the water pump shaft; the bearing requires no lubrication.

With any type of pressure cooling system, the first part of any cooling system check should begin with a complete pressure check of both the radiator and the pressure cap itself.

The recommended pressure cap of the Tiger is one of 13-15 lbs. p.s.i. The use of such a high pressure raises the boiling point of the coolant which is of great advantage in high altitudes and in tropical conditions.

It should also be noted that the cooling system of the Tiger cannot be completely drained if the car is fitted with a heater; thus if anti-freeze is going to be used in the car, make it a permanent type. Whenever the cooling system is drained for work on the engine, it is important that the heater controls be set to the **hot** position before refilling.

If the cooling system has been checked and the pressure cap and radiator are in good condition with no leaks in the radiator, hoses or cylinder head gaskets then the Tiger's overheating problems can generally be traced to the following causes.

CAUSES OF OVERHEATING:
 (1) Incorrect thermostat. Should be a 160°, pellet-type for summer, and a 180° for the winter.
 (2) Slipping fan belt.
 (3) Incorrect ignition advance, usually too much retard. Try setting advance to 9-12° BTDC @ 700 rpm engine idle speed.
 (4) Incorrect advance curve in distributor.
 (5) Cracked cylinder head or block.

A faulty thermostat can generally be detected by a slow engine warm-up plus overheating.

There is another cause of overheating in the Tiger that can be cured, but will cost a few dollars. The Tiger's engine is very snug in the engine compartment. The problem is that the air coming through the radiator can't get out.

The solution is to fit the optional fiberglass hood, which is Rootes (Sunbeam) part No. LAT-79. Its cost is $135.00 list. The other problem is that in slow moving traffic the standard equipment four-blade, 14" fan just isn't enough to do the job. The answer is to fit the LAT-80 six-bladed fiberglass fan. In almost 98% of the overheating cases, the correct ignition advance, the LAT-79 hood, and the correct thermostat will solve the problem.

POOR PERFORMANCE
 (1) Lean mixture: Clogged fuel filter, too small main jets, wrong setting on accelerator pump stroke mechanism.
 (2) Rich mixture: Too large main jets, automatic choke staying open, fuel percolating, fuel pump pressure too high (5 lbs. psi. correct), float level too high.

POOR GAS MILEAGE
  (1) main jets too large
  (2) too high fuel pump pressure
  (3) high float levels
  (4) idle mixture adjustment too rich
  (5) engine running too cold (use higher thermostat)
  (6) accelerator pump setting incorrect
  (7) clogged air cleaner

POOR ACCELERATION
  (1) power valve incorrect
  (2) float level too low
  (3) main jets too small
  (4) not getting full throttle
  (5) air-leaks into manifolds
  (6) choke not completely open
  (7) clogged air-cleaner
  (8) clogged gas-filter
  (9) clogged mufflers
  (10) incorrect ignition advance
  (11) improper sparkplugs or gap
  (12) On engines that have undergone camshaft or compression changes, poor acceleration can often be traced to too small carburetors, or restricted exhaust system.

POOR TOP-END PERFORMANCE
  (1) usually too small main jets
  (2) throttle linkage not correctly adjusted and/or failure to get full throttle opening
  (3) dirty, clogged air-cleaner filter, restricted air-intake to carburetor
  (4) restricted fuel line filter, fuel-pump filter, bent or restriction in fuel lines
  (5) excessive restriction in mufflers, bent or damaged tail pipes
  (6) carburetor accelerating pump incorrectly set or not working
  (7) carburetor float levels incorrectly set, too low generally allowing fuel to "run-away" from jets during hard acceleration
  (8) leak in floats, allowing fuel to sink float
  (9) if car is in operation at higher than normal altitudes, possibility of too rich jets and accelerating pump adjustment
  (10) faulty or incorrect power valve
  (11) fuel octane rating too low for engine performance
  (12) fuel pressure should be 5½ lbs. static, check fuel pump operation. The original S.U. pump can be replaced with a unit such as a Stewart-Warner. In this case use 6 lbs. static for the Holley carburetor
  (13) clogged metering passages, or wrong sized jets

Note: On all Tigers equipped with the Ford 2-bbl. carburetor fuel float level setting should be made using the "wet-level" setting. This is very important with the new resilient tipped needle as a dry level setting cannot be made.

The float level setting with the 4-bbl. Holley should also be made "wet".

On the Holley, check float level thru "sight plugs" on right side of carburetor with engine running at idle, fuel should be at the bottom of the opening. When adjusting float level, stop engine to prevent fire danger.

Check level after each adjustment.

Trouble shooting the battery system:

Many Tiger owners who live in warm or hot areas find that their batteries are in constant need of topping up or refilling. This can often be traced to an incorrect setting of the voltage regulator. The regulators are generally set for an ambient temperature setting of 80-85° F. (29.4° C.) Thus under higher under-the-hood temperatures the voltage output becomes too high, resulting in an overcharge of the battery.

The correct setting of the regulators can usually cure this constant filling up.

Correct setting of the Tiger regulator for the following under-the-hood (ambient) temperatures:

Ambient Temp. F°	Generator/Regulator settings
25°F and below	15.1/15.9
35	15.0/15.8
45	14.9/15.7
55	14.8/15.6
65	14.7/15.5
75	14.6/15.4
85	14.5/15.3
95	14.3/15.1
105	15.2/15.0
115	15.1/14.9
125	13.9/14.6
135	13.8/14.6
145	13.6/14.4
over 145°	Park it!

To correctly determine your car's under-the-hood temperature, mount a thermometer by the voltage regulator and check the temperature after about an hour's drive.

This setting should be made in the winter and again in the summer months. There are adjustable voltage regulators on the market that can be set by a dial for the high or low output settings. This type of regulator combined with a voltage meter on the dash would be a easy solution to the regulator problems.

SPARK PLUG NOTES

1. **NORMAL SERVICE SPARK PLUGS**
   SPARK PLUG EQUIVALENT AND HEAT RANGE CHART

HOT	*AUTOLITE	**CHAMPION	***AC
	BF-82	F14Y	86TS-85TS
	BF-42	F11Y	84TS*c.
	BF-32*a.	F9Y*b.	none
	BF-22	F83Y	none
COLD	BF-12	F62Y	none

   For colder ranges than BF-12 or F62Y see racing range below

   * AUTOLITE POWER-TIP
     *a. recommended normal service
   ** CHAMPION PROJECTED CORE
     *b. recommended normal service
   *** AC EXTENDED TIP
     *c. recommended normal service

2. **RACING SERVICE SPARK PLUGS**

HOT	AUTOLITE RACING GAP	CHAMPION RACING GAP
	BF703	F63R, F61R
	BF603	F58R
	BF403	F55T
COLD	BF203	F53T

   The Tiger 260 V-8 uses an 18mm tapered seat plug.
   No gasket is used on the Tiger 260 plugs.

3. **SPARK PLUG GAP**   Normal service recommendations;

Autolite BF-32	.032"	normal
Champion F9Y	.032"	
Autolite BF-22	.028"	cold
Champion F83Y	.028"	
Autolite BF-42	.035"	hot
Champion F11Y	.035"	

FACTORY OPTIONS

SUNBEAM TIGER-260
Factory Options

Part No.	Description	List Price
LAT-1*	Super induction kit — (Hi-Rise manifold and Holley 4-bbl. carb.)	$140.00
LAT-2	Dress-up kit — polished aluminum rocker covers, chrome air cleaner, radiator and oil filler cap.	$ 69.00
LAT-4	Large capacity aluminum oil pan.	$ 86.00
LAT-5	Traction-Master anti-tramp rods.	$ 42.25
LAT-7	Steel N.H.R.A. & A.H.R.A. approved scatter shield.	$100.00
LAT-8	Polished aluminum rocker arm covers.	$ 40.00
LAT-10	Tiger key chain.	$ 1.50
LAT-12	Tiger ash tray (for den or office).	$ .85
LAT-13	Tiger pocket lighter.	$ 1.50
LAT-14	Tiger embroidered jacket patch.	$ 2.00
LAT-15	Tiger flag set.	$ 3.00
LAT-16	Tiger decals.	$ .15
LAT-17	Men's Tiger "tee-shirts".	$ 1.70
LAT-18	Tiger rally jacket.	$ 8.50
LAT-20*	Hi-lift camshaft kit — complete, with ¾ solid lifter camshaft, 16 solid lifters, 16 outer, 16 inner valve springs, gaskets, one dual-point distributor.	$100.00

*The LAT-1 & LAT-20 kits are used on the 245 BHP engine.

The LAT-1 kit when supplied separately is fitted with a Holley No. 1-12 4-bbl. carburetor of 465 c.f.m. for use with the hydraulic lifter camshaft.

When the LAT-1 and LAT-20 kits are ordered as original equipment on the 245 BHP Tiger, the carburetor is a Holley R-3259-AS, 4-bbl. of 715 c.f.m.

Part No.	Description	List Price
LAT-21	Lightweight horns.	$ 15.00
LAT-22	7,000 R.P.M. tachometer	$ 55.00
LAT-25	Fiberglass hood air-scoop for fitting on standard hood.	$ 15.00
LAT-27	Cast-iron low restriction exhaust manifolds	$ 65.00

LAT-48	Jacket pocket patch Tiger.	$ .75
LAT-50	Limited-slip differential (must use LAT-51, 52, 53, 54 ring gear and pinion set).	$110.00
LAT-51	Crown wheel and pinion 3.07:1 ratio.	$ 50.00
LAT-52	3.31:1 ratio set.	$ 50.00
LAT-53	3.54:1 ratio set.	$ 50.00
LAT-54	3.73:1 ratio set.	$ 50.00
LAT-58	Chrome silver Tiger tail stripe kit.	$ 3.50
LAT-60	Heavy duty street clutch set, pressure plate and disc.	$ 50.50
LAT-63	Boy's "tee-shirt".	$ 1.50
LAT-67	Men's heavy sweat shirt	$ 3.00
LAT-70	Polished aluminum 5.50x13 wheels. each:	$ 48.00
LAT-73	Competition header kit.	$140.00
LAT-74	Low restriction exhaust muffler kit.	$ 52.00
LAT-76	Hi-speed HD shock absorber—rear	$ 16.85
LAT-77	Hi-speed HD front shocks.	$ 16.85
LAT-79	Lightweight, fiberglass hood, with air-scoop and engine heat exhaust outlets.	$135.00
LAT-80	Lightweight, fiberglass 6 blade engine fan, variable-pitch at high rpm for minimum drag.	

TORQUE SPECIFICATIONS

GENERAL TORQUE LOADING FIGURES
SUNBEAM TIGER V-8, 260 c.i.d.

TORQUE in ft. lbs.

ENGINE

Cylinder heads	68 lbs. ft.
Crankshaft, main bearing caps	65 lbs. ft.
Connecting rods (big end bearing caps)	44 lbs. ft.
Flywheel to crankshaft	80 lbs. ft.
Clutch, pressure plate to flywheel	
Stock or LAT-60 unit w/ 5/16" bolts	18 lbs. ft.
HAYS INVADER Competition unit w/ 3/8" bolts	30-35 lbs. ft.
Crankshaft vibration damper (pulley)	70-90 lbs. ft.
Intake manifold to cylinder heads	
Cast-iron intake manifold	14 lbs. ft.
Aluminum intake manifold	15 lbs. ft.
Exhaust manifolds and exhaust headers	16 lbs. ft.
Spark plugs	15-20 lbs. ft.
Valve cover bolts	3-5 lbs. ft.

GEARBOX, Ford HEH or HEE
Transmission to extension housing   46 lbs. ft.
Filler plug to case   15 lbs. ft.
Drain plug to case   25 lbs. ft.

REAR AXLE
Hypoid bevel pinion nut   125 lbs. ft.
Pinion bearing pre-load   10 lbs. ft.

For other chassis torque figures, see workshop manual.

RIBBON GAUGE CLEARANCES

Ribbon Gauge Piston Clearance Chart
Sunbeam Tiger V-8, 260 (3.80" bore)

Ribbon — 0.0015" Thick and 0.500" Wide

Pull lbs.	Clearance inches
7 lbs.	0.0002"
6	0.0004"
5	0.0007"
4	0.0009"
3	0.0012"
2	0.0015"
1	0.0017"
0	0.0020"

Ribbon — 0.002" Thick and 0.500" Wide

Pull lbs.	Clearance inches
9 lbs.	0.0002"
8	0.0005"
7	0.0007"
6	0.0010"
5	0.0012"
4	0.0015"
3	0.0017"
2	0.0020"
1	0.0022"
0	0.0025"

Ribbon — 0.0035" Thick and 0.500" Wide

Pull lbs.	Clearance inches
13 lbs.	0.0012"
12	0.0014"

Pull lbs.	Clearance inches
11	0.0016"
10	0.0018"
9	0.0021"
8	0.0023"
7	0.0025"
6	0.0027"
5	0.0030"
4	0.0032"
3	0.0033"
2	0.0036"
1	0.0038"
0	0.0040"

Ribbon — 0.006" Thick and 0.500" Wide

Pull lbs.	Clearance inches
13 lbs.	0.0038"
12	0.0040"
11	0.0041"
10	0.0043"
9	0.0045"
8	0.0047"
7	0.0049"
6	0.0050"
5	0.0057"
4	0.0059"
3	0.0060"
2	0.0062"
1	0.0063"
0	0.0065"

Note: When checking the piston to bore clearance, ribbon and piston fit must be snug in order to obtain an accurate reading. It is necessary to support the weight of the piston with one hand to prevent the piston from twisting in the bore of the block and giving an erroneous reading.

A used piston must always be checked in the bore from which it was removed.

Each piston should be marked with the cylinder number of the bore from which it was removed, and in the case of new pistons, mark them with their bore as they are fitted.

HOLLEY HI-PERFORMANCE CARBURETOR

There are two different Holley four-barrel carburetors used on the Tiger V-8 260. The standard carburetor supplied in the LAT-1 induction kit is the smallest in terms of cubic feet per minute air-flow rating (c.f.m.). This is the Holley 1-12. Model R-1848-B. The latter set of numbers will be found on the face of the air-horn as a "LIST-1848" number for carburetor identification.

The c.f.m. rating of this carburetor is 465. This is sufficient for the stock unmodified Tiger 260, with either the standard hydraulic-lifter camshaft or the solid tappet LAT-20 camshaft for street use. For competition purposes, however, you will have to use the optional Holley R-3259-1AAS carburetor which has a 715 c.f.m. rating.

The tuning of the Holley four-barrel carburetor is actually a very simple process. The jet sizes can be changed in a matter of minutes by removing the two end float bowls.

These are shown in the illustration on page 88-89 as items No. 72 and No. 77.

The primary system uses two Holley screw-in type jets, while the secondary system of the Holley 1-12 uses a metering body plate.

The jets in the Holley 1-12 primary system must be replaced in matched pairs, and the secondary metering jet plate is replaced as required.

Specifications for the Holley 1-12

Main jet—primary .... No. 57*
Main jet—secondary .... none
Main jet metering plate—secondary 34R-2007-3*
Power valve .... No. 85*
Air vent clearance at idle .... .050" - .070"
Pump override spring adjustment .... .015" min.
Pump stroke-position
    Summer, 70°F and over .... No. 1 hole
    Winter, 70°F and below .... No. 2 hole
Fuel level, engine warm at idle & level
    Primary .... bottom of sight plug
    Secondary .... bottom of sight plug
Fuel pressure at fuel inlet .... 5 p.s.i.
Float level when overhauling carburetor
    (Use Kent-Moore tool No. 10-192)

Primary .... 7/8"
Secondary .... 9/16"

*These are Holley numbers found stamped on jets, metering plates and power valves.

The larger of the two Holleys is the model R-3259-1AAS. This carburetor, designed for maximum competition use on the Tiger 260 with a LAT-20 camshaft and LAT-1 hi-rise intake manifold, has a rating of 715 c.f.m. air-flow. Its operation and tuning is like that of the smaller Holley 1-12. The differences between the two carburetors in jet sizes are as follow. The Holley R-3259-1AAS uses, in place of a secondary metering plate, a secondary jet body similar to the primary body used in both the Holley 1-12 and R-3259 carburetors, and thus uses the same type of screw-in jets in the secondary stage as it does in the primary.

Specifications of the Holley R-3259-1AAS
Main jet—primary .... No. 68
Main jet—secondary .... No. 78
Main jet metering plate—secondary ...... none
Power valve .... No. 85
Other tuning specifications same as Holley 1-12.

The Holley Jet Numbers stamped on the jets are a gas flow rating, NOT the size of the jet.

To enrichen a carburetor mixture, use a larger numbered jet, i.e., stock jet No. 68, one step richer would be to use a No. 69 jet, two steps richer would be to use a No. 70 jet.

To lean out a mixture, use the smaller size or numbered jets, i.e., stock jet No. 68, one step lean would be to use a No. 67, two steps lean would be to use a No. 66.

In the case of the secondary metering plate used in the Holley 1-12, the stock plate is No. 34R-2007-3, one step rich would be 34R-2007-4, lean would be -2.

SPECIAL PARTS NUMBERS

Special Parts For The Tiger. The following parts are often needed when working on the Tiger 260.

Part No.	Supply No.	No. Needed
Engine		
Intake manifold gasket set	(Ford No.)	
Manifold to cylinder head	C20Z-9441-A	2

Seal—front		C20Z-9A425-A	1
Seal—rear		C20Z-9A424-A	1
Cylinder head gasket		(Ford No.)	
Stock 260		C20Z-6051-C	2
Special Thin*		C5ZZ-6051-A	2*

*Only if the engine can use this gasket (see text).

Valve cover gasket set		(Ford No.)	
		C20Z-6584-A	2
Oil filter gasket		(Sunbeam No.)	
(needed when changing filter)		9078049	1
Complete engine gasket sets		(Ford No.)	
Complete engine		C20Z-6008-C	1
Valve grind set		C20Z-6079-C	1

Carburetor

Ford two-barrel carburetor		(Ford No.)	
Gasket set	Carb. No. C4DF-F	C20Z-9502-B	1
	Carb. No. C4DF-N	C20Z-9502-C	1
Tune-up kit	Carb. No. C4DF-F	C3AZ-9A586-B	1
	Carb. No. C4DF-N	C4DZ-9A586-A	1
Repair kit	Carb. No. C4DF-F	C3AZ-9590-C	1
	Carb. No. C4DF-N	C4DZ-9590-A	1
Holley No. 1-12 carburetor		(Holley No.)	
Gasket kit		4-4	1
Needle and seat		6-6	2
Pump plunger		8-153	1
Float		16R-266A	2
Street fuel bowl		85B-1351(P)	1
		85B-1350(S)	1
Competition fuel bowl*		34R-5057A(P)	1*
		34R-5065A(S)	1*

*This fuel bowl may require some re-working of the firewall on some cars; check fit.

Main jet, standard, primary	22-R-40-57	2
Main jet, standard, secondary	34-R-2007-3	1
Power valve	25-R-219A-85	1
Master kit	85-R-648	1
Holley R-3259 carburetor	(Holley No.)	
Gasket kit	4-184	1
Needle and seat	6-73	2
Pump plunger	8-153	1
Float	16R-393A-3	2
Street fuel bowl	34R-4235A (P)	1
	34R-4557A (S)	1
Competition fuel bowl*	34R-5057A (P)	1*

34R-5065A (S)		1*

*These fuel bowls may require some re-working of the firewall on some cars; check fit.

Main jet, standard, primary	22R-40-68	2
Main jet, standard, secondary ..	22R-40-78	2
Power valve	25R-237A-85	1
Master kit	85R-2514	1

The following parts references may prove helpful.

Gasket, timing cover to block	(Ford No.) C40Z-6020-A	1
Water pump unit	(Ford No.) C4JE-8501-A	1
Housing gasket	(Ford No.) C20Z-8507-B	1
By-pass hose	(Ford No.) C20Z-8597-A	1
Water outlet pipe (top)	(Ford No.) C30Z-8594-B	1
Gasket for above	(Ford No.) C30Z-8255-A	1
Fanbelt, standard	(Ford No.) C20Z-8620-E	1
Radiator hoses	(Sunbeam No.)	
Upper	1224840	1
Lower	1224841	1
Radiator to header tank	1224842	1
Steam pipe to header tank	1224843	1

SPEEDOMETER CORRECTION

To correct for various final drive gear ratios use the following; w/ 23.5" tire

Gear	MPH per 1000 RPM
2.88:1	23.5
3.31:1	20.5
3.73:1	18.2
4.86:1	13.9

Note: The above figures are only approximately accurate and should not be used for Rally corrections. They should serve as a guide for selecting gear ratios.

The correct MPH per 1000 RPM should be plotted on your own car with carefully measured tire sizes and an accurate tachometer.

It should be pointed out that many Tigers have tachometers that read slightly high. The average Tiger with 2.88:1 gears and original equipment tires such as the Dunlop RS-5 5.90x13 has a slight speedometer error due to the small tire size, the high final drive ratio, the available speedometer drive and transmission shaft speedometer gear.

The transmission fitted to the Tiger is the American-built Ford (early models Warner T-10), the speedometer is a Smith unit, and the final drive ring gear and pinion an English unit. There are, therefore, three factors that prevent a correct reading.

This can be overcome by two methods. One, having the speedometer head re-calibrated and using a different set of speedometer drive gears (both the speedometer cable gear and the transmission output shaft gear). This is an expensive way to go since it requires pulling the transmission to remove the tail shaft.

The second is to have the rear tires changed to a 7.00x13 size, and use a Mustang set of speedometer 2.80:1 drive cable gears which are 14 tooth units, rather than the 15 tooth type that are original equipment. This should give you a speedometer that will read approximately 3% slow, resulting in the following figures: Speedometer reading: 60 MPH; true speed: 61.8 MPH — as against the original Tiger speedometer error which would read 60 MPH with a true speed of 56.2 MPH.

A few Tigers have been made using a 3.34:1 final drive gear ratio in place of the standard 2.88:1. There is no service bulletin out on this so no chassis numbers are available.

Always before checking speedometers, have the tach checked for correct readings and corrections noted.

SPEEDOMETER PLOT

Road speed/engine rpm: @ 1000 engine rpm w/2.88:1 final drive

Gearbox:	Ford HEH-E		HEH-B	
Gear	Ratio	mph/rpm	Ratio	mph/rpm
1st	2.32:1	10.31	2.78:1	8.61
2nd	1.69:1	14.17	1.93:1	12.41
3rd	1.29:1	18.56	1.36:1	17.36
4th	1.0:1	23.92	1.0:1	23.92

All below plots based on HEH-E transmission ratios.

Corrective speeds: w/2.88:1 final drive, based on 24.5" tire 4th Gear:

Engine rpm	mph
2000 rpm	51 mph
2500 rpm	63 mph
3000 rpm	76 mph
3400 rpm	80 mph

Corrective speeds: w/3.34:1 final drive gear based on 24.5" tire 4th Gear:

Engine rpm	mph
2000 rpm	44 mph
2300 rpm	50 mph
2500 rpm	55 mph
2750 rpm	60 mph
3000 rpm	65 mph

3700 rpm   80 mph

Speedometer error: Based on Road & Track Road Test
Indicated mph   **True mph**
30 mph   28.1 mph
40 mph   37.5 mph
60 mph   56.2 mph
80 mph   75.0 mph

To compute plot based on the HEH-E Transmission Ratios:
Use a known measured mile; first run the mile to check the accurate readings of the distance odometer. If the odometer checks out correct to the 1/10th of the measured mile distance, the following scale may be used to check the speedometer vs true mph.

	@ 20 mph	25	30	40	60	65
1 tenth mile = 0:18 min:sec		0:15	0:12	0:09	0:06	-
5 tenth mile = 1:30 min:sec		1:12	1:00	0:45	0:30	-
1 mile - min:sec		-	2:00	1:30	1:00	0:55

	@ 70 mph	75	80
1 tenth mile	-	-	-
5 tenth mile	-	-	-
1 mile = 0:53.5		0:52	0:45

Acceptable Speedometer error
Based on 2.88:1 final drive
24.5" tires

                   3% Fast
     Speedo: True:
     50 mph   48.5 mph
     60 mph   58.2 mph
     70 mph   67.9 mph
                   3% Slow
     Speedo: True:
     50 mph   51.5 mph
     60 mph   61.8 mph
     70 mph   72.1 mph

Plot Maximum Speed of Tiger w/ 4400 RPM limit top gear

Gear:	2.88:1	3.34:1	3.54:1	3.76:1
MPH:	112	96	90	85

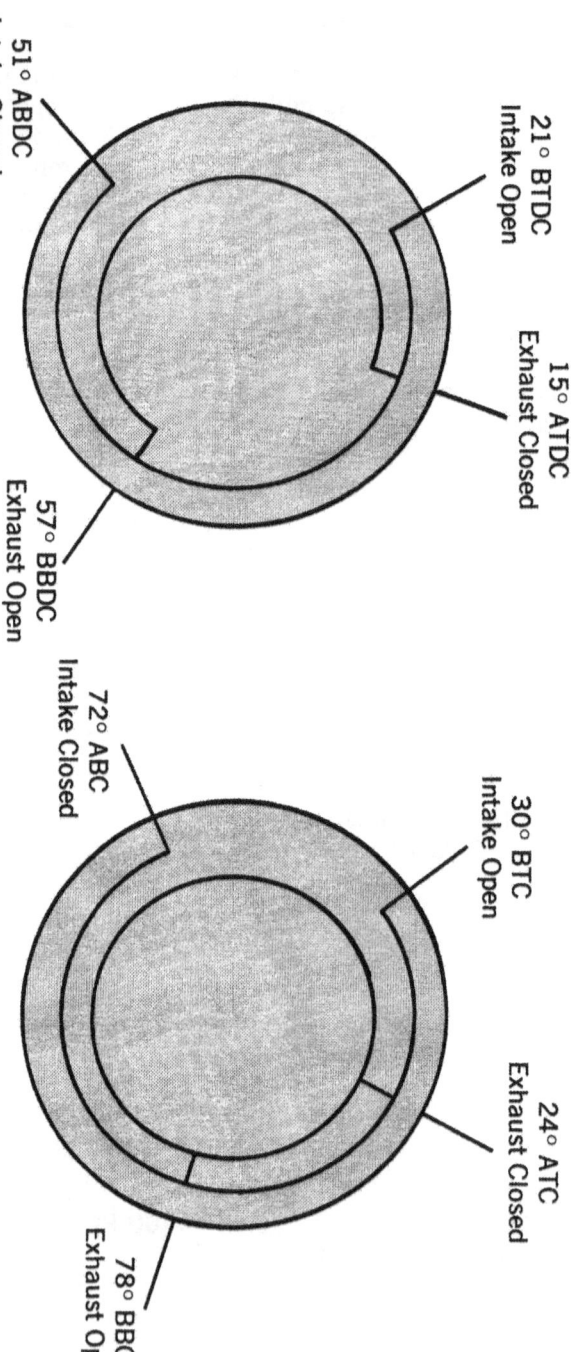

Top diagram:
- 21° BTDC Intake Open
- 15° ATDC Exhaust Closed
- 57° BBDC Exhaust Open
- 51° ABDC Intake Closed

164 BHP engine with hydraulic camshaft. Overlap: 36° Duration: 252° Lift: .380" @ 0 lash

Bottom diagram:
- 30° BTC Intake Open
- 24° ATC Exhaust Closed
- 78° BBC Exhaust Open
- 72° ABC Intake Closed

245 BHP engine with LAT-20 camshaft. Overlap: 54° Duration: 282° Lift: .457" @ .020 lash

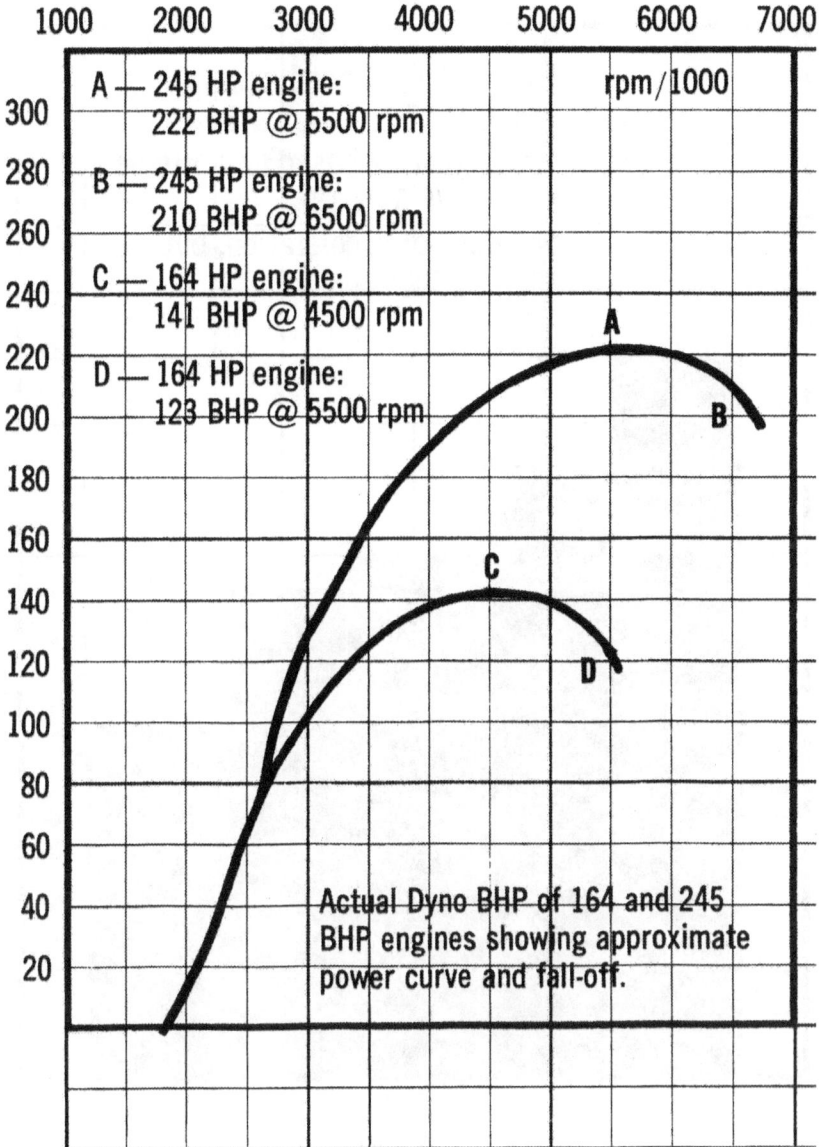

Potential Top Speed mph with 2.88:1, 3.07:1, 3.54:1 & 3.73:1 & 4.55:1 gearing based on a tire height of 24.5" (6.50 x 13)
Scale is not acceleration, but top MPH @ 6000 rpm

- 150 mph: 2.88:1 @ 6000 rpm
- 135 mph: 3.07:1 @ 6000 rpm
- 120 mph: 3.54:1 @ 6000 rpm
- 115 mph: 3.73:1 @ 6000 rpm
- 95 mph: 4.55:1 @ 6000 rpm

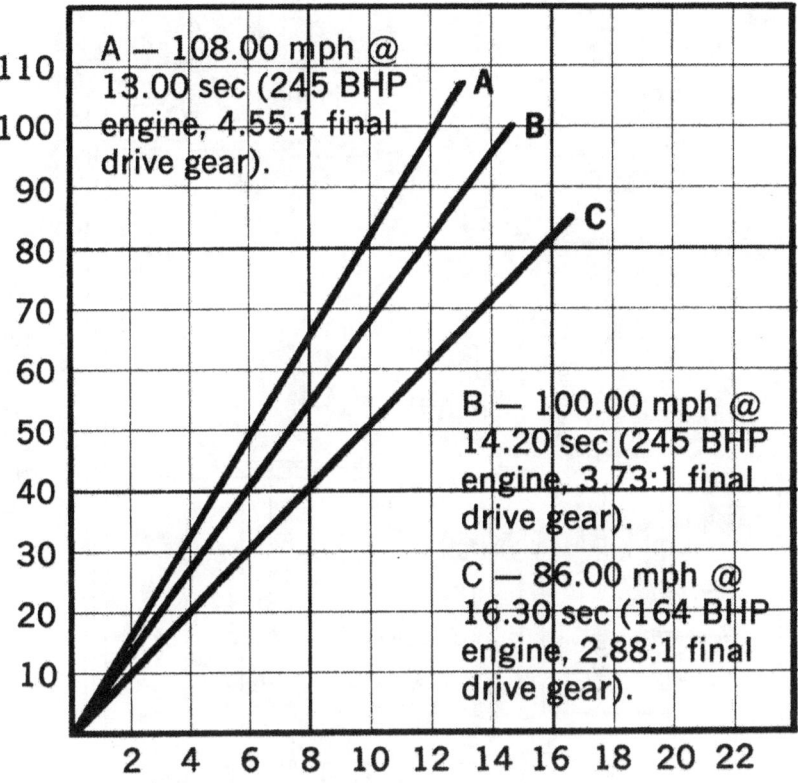

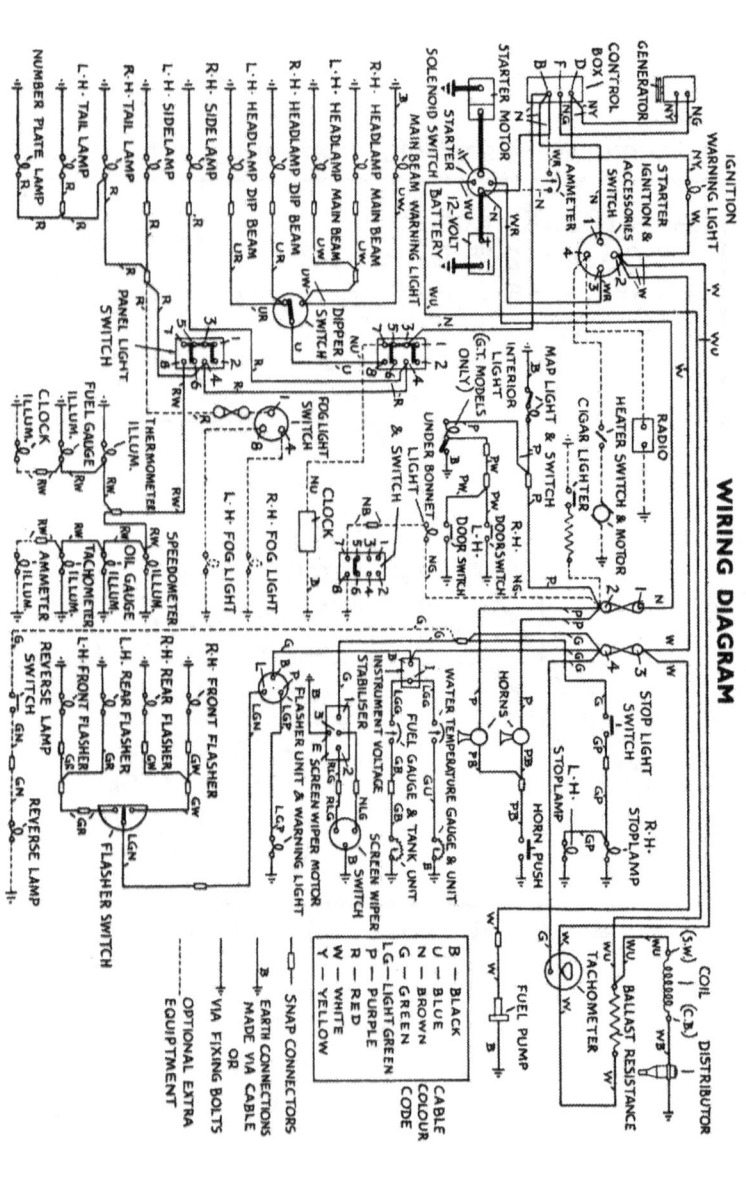

260 TIGER FLAT RATE TABLES

COOLING SYSTEM A

1. RADIATOR

Operation No.		Hrs.	Mins.
A-1/1	Block—R. & R.	1	30
A-1/2	Radiator drain tap—R. & R.	–	5
A-1/3	Cylinder block drain tap—R. & R. (one only)	–	25
A-1/4	Header tank—R. & R.	–	10
A-1/5	Fan Cowl—R. & R.	–	20

2. HOSES

Operation No.		Hrs.	Mins.
A-2/1	Radiator top hose—R. & R.	–	10
A-2/3	Radiator bottom hose—R. & R.	–	20
A-2/4	Header tank hose (top)—R. & R.	–	5
A-2/5	Header tank hose (bottom)—R. & R.	–	10

3. WATER PUMP AND FAN

Operation No.		Hrs.	Mins.
A-3/1	Pump and fan assembly—R. & R.	1	20
A-3/2	Pump—overhaul	1	32
A-3/3	Thermostat cover/thermostat—R. & R.	–	15
A-3/5	Fan—R. & R.	–	35
A-3/6	Fan pulley—R. & R.	–	40
A-3/7	Fan belt—R. & R. (including adjust)	–	10
A-3/8	Fan belt—adjust	–	5

ENGINE B

1. GENERAL

Operation No.		Hrs.	Mins.
B-1/3	Decarbonise (including grind in valves, set tappet clearances, plug points and contact breaker gap)	17	6
B-1/4	Inspect and measure cylinder bores (pistons out)	1	0
B-1/5	Complete engine—R. & R.	9	15

2. CYLINDER HEADS

Operation No.		Hrs.	Mins.
B-2/1	Rocker cover and joint—R. & R. (R.H. side)	1	10
B-2/1A	Rocker cover and joint—R. & R. (L.H. side)	–	30
B-2/2	Check holding nuts/bolts for torque loading	2	45
B-2/3	Cylinder head assembly—R. & R. (R.H. side)	8	39
B-2/3A	Cylinder head assembly—R. & R. (L.H. side)	8	57
B-2/3B	Cylinder head assemblies—R. & R. (both sides)	13	0

ENGINE B

Operation No.	7. CRANKSHAFT	Hrs.	Mins.
B-7/1	Flywheel and ring gear—R. & R.	10	3
B-7/3	Crankshaft—R. & R.	13	45
B-7/4	Inspect front, centre or rear main bearings—R. & R.—if necessary	3	6
B-7/5	Crankshaft pulley—R. & R.	1	59
B-7/6	Crankshaft damper—R. & R.	2	7

Operation No.	8. LUBRICATION SYSTEM	Hrs.	Mins.
B-8/1	Oil sump—R. & R.	1	12
B-8/2	Oil pump—R. & R.	1	18
B-8/3	Oil pump—overhaul	1	30
B-8/6	Oil filter element—R. & R.	–	20
B-8/7	Pressure relief valve—R. & R.	1	18
B-8/8	Crankcase ventilating system—to clean and check	–	24

Operation No.	9. CYLINDER BLOCK	Hrs.	Mins.
B-9/1	Cylinder block—R. & R. (Including transfer both heads, auxiliaries, etc.)	18	51

ENGINE B

Operation No.	10. MANIFOLDS	Hrs.	Mins.
B-10/1	Exhaust manifold—R. & R. (R.H. side)	8	53
B-10/1A	Exhaust manifold—R. & R. (L.H. side)	9	11
B-10/3	Inlet manifold—R. & R.	3	53

Operation No.	11. IGNITION SYSTEM	Hrs.	Mins.
B-11/1	Set of sparking plugs—R. & R. (fit new set)—Cold	–	36
B-11/1A	Set of sparking plugs—R. & R. (fit new set)—Hot	–	55
B-11/2	Clean plugs and test—Cold	–	56
B-11/2A	Clean plugs and test—Hot	1	15
B-11/3	One H.T. lead—R. & R.	–	3
B-11/4	Distributor—R. & R.	–	24
B-11/5	Distributor—clean points, set gap, etc.	–	48
B-11/6	Coil—R. & R.	–	18
B-11/7	Capillary vacuum tube—R. & R.	–	10
B-11/8	Distributor cap—R. & R.—Renew or change over H.T. leads	–	18

Operation No.	12. ENGINE SUPPORTS	Hrs.	Mins.
B-12/1	Front support—R. & R. (one)	–	50
B-12/2	Rear support—R. & R.	–	30

ENGINE B

3. VALVE GEAR

Operation No.		Hrs.	Mins.
B-3/1	Reset tappet clearances (both sides)	2	10
B-3/2	Rocker arm stud—R. & R. (L.H. side)	–	45
B-3/2A	Rocker arm stud—R. & R. (R.H. side)	1	25
B-3/3	Rocker arm—R. & R. (one) (L.H. side)	–	40
B-3/3A	Rocker arm—R. & R. (one) (R.H. side)	1	20
B-3/3B	Rocker arm—R. & R. (all)	3	10
B-3/4	One valve/valve spring—R. & R. (R.H. side) Nos. 6 to 7	2	8
B-3/5	Each additional valve/valve spring to B-3/5—R. & R.	–	20
B-3/6	One valve/valve spring—R. & R. (L.H. side) No. 1 to 7	1	32
B-3/7	Each additional valve/valve spring to B-3/6	–	20
B-3/8	One valve/valve spring—R. & R. (No. 8 L.H. side)	9	12
B-3/9	One valve/valve spring—R. & R. (No. 8 R.H. side)	8	54
B-3/11	Hydraulic tappets—R. & R. (R.H. side)	5	53
B-3/11A	Hydraulic tappets—R. & R. (L.H. side)	5	14
B-3/13	Push rod—R. & R. (Nos. 1 to 7 L.H. side)	1	17
B-3/13A	Push rods—R. & R. (Nos. 1 to 7 R.H. side)	1	53
B-3/13B	Push rod—R. & R. (No. 8 L.H. side)	8	57
B-3/13C	Push rod—R. & R. (No. 8 R.H. side)	8	39

ENGINE B

4. CAMSHAFT AND TIMING GEAR

Operation No.		Hrs.	Mins.
B-4/1	Timing cover (engine in car)—R. & R.	2	36
B-4/2	Camshaft sprocket—R. & R.	2	45
B-4/3	Crankshaft sprocket—R. & R.	2	45
B-4/4	Timing chain—R. & R.	2	45
B-4/6	Camshaft—R. & R.	11	18
B-4/7	Camshaft bearings—R. & R.	13	45

5. PISTONS

B-5/1	One piston—R. & R. (R.H. side)	10	39
B-5/1A	One piston—R. & R. (L.H. side)	11	3
B-5/2	Each additional piston to B-5/1—R. & R. and B-5 1A	–	20
B-5/3	Measure bores and fit new set of pistons	16	52

6. CONNECTING RODS

B-6/1	One con rod—R. & R.	10	39
B-6/2	Each additional rod to B-6/1—R. & R.	–	20
B-6/5	Big end bearings—R. & R.	1	48

FUEL SYSTEM C

1. CARBURETTOR

Operation No.		Hrs. Mins.
C-1/1	Air cleaner—R. & R. (*Including clean or renew element*) ...	- 10
C-1/3	Clean, check and tune carburettor on motor ...	- 30
C-1/4	Carburettor—R. & R. ...	- 36
C-1/5	Carburettor float chamber filter—Clean ...	- 15

2. FUEL PUMP

C-2/1	Fuel pump—R. & R. (includes drain) ...	- 35
C-2/4	Fuel pump—check output ...	- 15

FUEL SYSTEM C

3. FUEL LINES

Operation No.		Hrs. Mins.
C-3/1	Pipe, tank to pump—R. & R. (*Includes drain fuel tank*)	- 15
C-3/3	Pipe, pump to carburettor—R. & R. ...	- 20
C-3/4	Blow out fuel lines (*Includes drain fuel tank*) ...	- 15
C-3/5	Balance pipe complete—R. & R. ...	- 20
C-3/6	Fuel filter element renew ...	- 18

4. FUEL TANK

C-4/1	Fuel tank—R. & R. (one) ...	1 0
C-4/2	Flush out tank additional to C-4/1 (each) ...	- 10
C-4/3	Fuel gauge tank unit—R. & R. ...	- 20
C-4/4	Filler neck—R. & R. ...	- 35
C-4/5	Rubber hose—R. & R. ...	- 35
C-4/6	Grommet (filler neck/rear panel)—R. & R.	- 35

CLUTCH & PROPELLOR SHAFT D

Operation No.		Hrs. Mins.
	1. CLUTCH CONTROLS	
D-1/2	Master cylinder—R. & R. ...	1 0
D-1/3	Master cylinder—overhaul ...	1 30
D-1/4	Hydraulic pipe (reservoir to cylinder)—R. & R.	– 35
D-1/5	Slave cylinder—R. & R. ...	– 30
D-1/6	Slave cylinder—overhaul ...	– 40
D-1/7	Bleed hydraulic system ...	– 15
D-1/9	Pedal—R. & R. ...	– 20
	2. CLUTCH UNIT	
D-2/1	Driven plate—R. & R. ...	9 51
D-2/2	Clutch cover assembly—R. & R.	9 51
D-2/4	Withdrawal lever—R. & R. ...	10 27
D-2/5	Roller release bearing—R. & R.	10 9
D-2/7	Bellhousing—R. & R. ...	9 39
	3. PROPELLER SHAFT	
D-3/1	Propeller shaft assembly—R. & R.	– 15
D-3/2	Propeller shaft assembly—overhaul	1 30

TRANSMISSION & CONTROLS E

Operation No.		Hrs. Mins.
	1. GEARBOX CONTROLS	
E-1/14	Gear lever—R. & R. ...	– 20
E-1/15	Reverse operating rod—R. & R.	– 30
E-1/16	1st and 2nd operating rod—R. & R.	– 30
E-1/17	3rd and 4th operating rod—R. & R.	– 30
E-1/18	Side cover—R. & R. (Warner)	1 20
E-1/19	Top cover—R. & R. (Ford)	9 30
	2. GEARBOX UNIT	
E-2/1	Complete unit—R. & R. ...	9 15
E-2/2	Complete unit—overhaul ...	11 39

FRONT SUSPENSION F

Operation No.	1. INSPECTION AND ADJUSTMENTS	Hrs.	Mins.
F-1/1	Camber angle and track (toe-in)—Inspect ...	-	50
F-1/2	Camber angle and track—adjust ...	1	30
F-1/3	Track (toe-in)—adjust ...	-	30
F-1/4	One front hub—inspect end float ...	-	10
F-1/5	One front hub—adjust end float ...	-	15

Operation No.	2. FRONT SUSPENSION UNIT	Hrs.	Mins.
F-2/1	Anti-roll bar—R. & R. ...	-	45
F-2/2	*Front suspension unit complete—R. & R. ...	1	53
F-2/3	*Crossmember—R. & R. (*Including* remove unit, strip, transfer linkages, etc.) ...	4	58
F-2/4	*Top wishbone—R. & R. ...	1	55

FRONT SUSPENSION F

Operation No.	Front Suspension Unit—*continued*	Hrs.	Mins.
F-2/5	*Top swivel bearing—R. & R. ...	1	15
F-2/6	*Axle carrier—R. & R. ...	1	20
F-2/9	*Bottom wishbone—R. & R. ...	1	30
F-2/11	Shock absorber—R. & R. ...	-	20
F-2/12	Coil spring—R. & R. ...	1	5
F-2/13	Rebound rubber—R. & R. ...	-	25
F-2/14	Bump rubber—R. & R. ...	-	10
F-2/15	Hub—R. & R. (*also see* Disc Brake Section) ...	-	25
F-2/16	One wheel stud—R. & R. ...	-	30
F-2/17	Each additional stud to F-2/16—R. & R. ...	-	5

*When new parts are installed the times for camber and track inspection or adjustment are to be added to these times.

REAR AXLE G
REAR SUSPENSION H
STEERING J

Operation No.	G. REAR AXLE	Hrs.	Mins.	Operation No.	H. REAR SUSPENSION	Hrs.	Mins.
	1. COMPLETE UNIT				**1. REAR SPRINGS**		
G-1/1	Complete axle assembly—R. & R.	3	1	H-1/1	Inspect spring camber	—	25
G-1/4	One axle shaft—R. & R.	2	30	H-1/2	One spring—R. & R.	—	50
G-1/5	One hub—R. & R. (including shimming)	2	0	H-1/3	One spring—overhaul	1	50
G-1/6	One wheel stud—R. & R.	2	0	H-1/4	One spring eye bush—R. & R.	1	15
G-1/7	Each additional wheel stud to G-1/6—R. & R.	—	5	H-1/5	One frame bush—R. & R.	—	45
G-1/8	One shaft bearing—R. & R.	2	30	H-1/6	One bump rubber—R. & R.	—	15
G-1/9	Axle shaft seal—R. & R.	2	30	H-1/8	Panhard rod—R. & R.	—	30
				H-1/9	Panhard rod—adjust	—	30
	2. DIFFERENTIAL UNIT				**2. SHOCK ABSORBERS**		
G-2/1	Complete unit—R. & R.	9	1	H-2/1	One rear shock absorber—R. & R.	—	20
G-2/2	Complete unit—overhaul	10	1		**J. STEERING**		
G-2/3	Pinion oil seal—R. & R.	1	0		**1. HANDWHEEL, CONTROLS, ETC.**		
				J-1/1	Horn ring—R. & R.	—	5
				J-1/2	Handwheel—R. & R.	—	25
				J-1/3	Steering column cowl—R. & R.	—	10
				J-1/4	Indicator control (with wiring)—R. & R.	—	15

STEERING J
BRAKES K

2. STEERING UNIT

Operation No.		Hrs.	Mins.
J-2/1	Complete steering rack—R. & R.	2	50
J-2/5	Complete column—R. & R.	1	20
J-2/6	Complete column—overhaul	2	13

3. LINKAGES

Operation No.		Hrs.	Mins.
J-3/6	*Ball joint—outer—R. & R.	–	20

*To include camber and track inspection and adjustment when new parts are installed (Refer to Section F–1 for additional times).

K. BRAKES

1. ADJUSTMENTS

Operation No.		Hrs.	Mins.
K-1/1	Adjust brakes	–	15
K-1/2	Bleed brakes at four wheels	–	30
K-1/3	Tighten all hydraulic connections	–	15
K-1/4	Adjust handbrake free travel	–	15
K-1/5	Blow-out brake drums	–	15

BRAKES K

2. BACK PLATES AND DRUMS

Operation No.		Hrs.	Mins.
K-2/1	One brake drum—R. & R.	–	10
K-2/2	Regrind one brake drum	–	25
K-2/3	Fit relined shoes (one wheel)	–	45
K-2/4	Pull-off springs (one wheel)—R. & R.	–	15
K-2/5	Wheel cylinder (one wheel)—R. & R.	1	0
K-2/6	Wheel cylinder (one wheel)—overhaul	1	15
K-2/9	Backing plate (one rear wheel)—R. & R.	1	30
K-2/11	Complete braking system—overhaul	6	30
K-2/12	One front or rear flexible hose—R. & R.	–	45

3. PEDALS AND LINKAGES

Operation No.		Hrs.	Mins.
K-3/1	Master cylinder—R. & R.	1	0
K-3/2	Master cylinder—overhaul	1	30
K-3/3	Stop light switch—R. & R.	–	45
K-3/4	Pedal—R. & R.	–	20

BRAKES K

4. HANDBRAKE

Operation No.		Hrs.	Mins.
K-4/1	Handbrake lever—R. & R. (*Including re-adjust cable*)	–	30
K-4/2	Handbrake cable—R. & R.	–	30
K-4/3	Cross shaft assembly—R. & R.	–	30
K-4/4	Cross shaft assembly—overhaul	1	0

5. DISC BRAKES

Operation No.		Hrs.	Mins.
K-5/1	One brake unit complete—R. & R. (one wheel)	1	15
K-5/2	One brake unit complete—overhaul (one wheel)	2	15
K-5/3	One disc—R. & R.	–	45
K-5/4	Renew piston seals (one unit)	–	35
K-5/5	Renew brake pads (both wheels)	–	15
K-5/6	Servo unit—R. & R.	–	45

TYRES & WHEELS L
EXHAUST SYSTEM M
ELECTRICAL SYSTEM N

L. TYRES AND WHEELS

Operation No.		Hrs.	Mins.
L-1/1	Re-balance two wheels. (5 wheels 1½ hours)	–	35
L-1/2	Transpose five wheels	–	30

M. EXHAUST SYSTEM

Operation No.		Hrs.	Mins.
M-1/1	Complete system from manifold—R. & R.	1	26
M-1/2	Exhaust pipe (from manifold R.H. side)—R. & R.	–	54
M-1/3	Exhaust pipe (from manifold L.H. side)—R. & R.	–	54
M-1/4	Silencer—R. & R. (R.H. side)	–	54
M-1/4A	Silencer—R. & R. (L.H. side)	–	54
M-1/6	Adjust suspension of complete system	1	0
M-1/7	One hanger assembly—R. & R.	–	15

N. ELECTRICAL SYSTEM

1. GENERATOR

Operation No.		Hrs.	Mins.
N-1/1	Complete unit—R. & R.	–	18
N-1/2	Complete unit—overhaul	1	12
N-1/3	Brushes—R. & R.	–	30
N-1/4	Pulley and cooling fan—R. & R.	–	10

ELECTRICAL SYSTEM N

Operation No.		Hrs. Mins.
	2. STARTER	
N-2/1	Complete unit—R. & R.	– 18
N-2/2	Starter drive—R. & R.	– 30
N-2/3	Brushes—R. & R.	– 54
N-2/4	Solenoid switch—R. & R.	– 50
	3. BATTERY	
N-3/1	Battery—R. & R.	– 15
N-3/2	Battery support—R. & R.	– 5
N-3/3	Cable—battery to starter solenoid—R. & R.	– 50
N-3/4	Cable—battery to earth—R. & R.	– 20
	4. WINDSCREEN WIPERS	
N-4/1	Motor unit and inner cable—R. & R.	– 35
N-4/2	Gearbox (one side)—R. & R.	– 45
N-4/3	Gearbox (both sides)—R. & R.	1 0
N-4/4	One wiper spindle grommet—R. & R.	– 5
N-4/5	Grommet—drive to bulkhead—R. & R.	– 15
	5. LAMPS	
N-5/1	Adjust alignment of headlamps	– 15
N-5/2	Headlamp lens unit—R. & R.	– 15
N-5/3	Complete headlamp assembly—R. & R.	– 30
N-5/4	One side lamp assembly—R. & R.	– 15
N-5/5	One stop/tail/flasher lamp assembly—R. & R.	– 10
N-5/6	One stop/tail/flasher lamp lens—R. & R.	– 15
N-5/7	Number plate lamp assembly—R. & R.	– 5
N-5/8	Roof lamp—R. & R. (G.T. only)	– 5
N-5/9	Dipswitch—R. & R.	– 10
	6. INSTRUMENT AND PANEL LAMPS	
N-6/1	One warning lamp bulb—R. & R.	– 5
N-6/2	Speedometer or rev. counter bulb—R. & R.	– 10
N-6/3	Ammeter, thermometer, fuel gauge or oil pressure gauge bulb—R. & R.	– 10

ELECTRICAL SYSTEM N

Operation No.		Hrs.	Mins.
	7. HORN AND FLASHER UNIT		
	(For horn ring and direction indicator switch see Section J, Page 11)		
N-7/1	Horn—R. & R.—low note (left-hand) ...	—	5
N-7/2	Horn—R. & R.—high note (right hand) ...	—	5
N-7/4	Flasher unit—R. & R. ...	—	5
	8. VOLTAGE REGULATOR AND FUSES		
N-8/1	Regulator—check voltage settings ...	—	15
N-8/2	Regulator and cut-out assembly—R. & R. ...	—	15
N-8/3	Fuse box—R. & R. ...	—	10
	9. INSTRUMENTS		
N-9/1	Rev. counter—R. & R. ...	—	20
N-9/2	Speedometer—R. & R. ...	—	20
N-9/3	Thermometer—R. & R. ...	—	20
N-9/4	Fuel gauge—R. & R. ...	—	20
N-9/5	Ammeter—R. & R. ...	—	20

ELECTRICAL SYSTEM N

Operation No.		Hrs.	Mins.
	9. Instruments—continued		
N-9/6	Oil pressure gauge—R. & R. ...	—	20
N-9/7	Complete instrument panel assembly—R. & R.	1	35
N-9/8	Instrument panel—R. & R. (Including change over all instruments)	2	45
N-9/9	Instrument voltage stabilizer—R. & R.	—	15
	10. CONTROL SWITCHES		
N-10/1	Ignition/starter control—R. & R.	—	20
N-10/4	Side/head lamp switch—R. & R.	—	30
N-10/5	Windscreen wiper switch—R. & R.	—	15
N-10/6	Panel lamp switch—R. & R.	—	15
N-10/7	Ventilator control (with cable)—R. & R.	—	15
	11. WIRING HARNESS		
N-11/1	Body harness—R. & R.	3	30
N-11/2	Chassis harness—R. & R. (Add 30 mins. if radio fitted)	3	30

BODY O

O. BODY

Operation No.		Hrs.	Mins.
1. BUMPERS AND AIR INTAKE GRILLE			
O-1/1	Front bumper assembly—R. & R.	—	10
O-1/2	Front bumper supports—R. & R.	—	20
O-1/3	Rear bumper assembly—R. & R.	—	10
O-1/4	Rear bumper supports—R. & R.	—	20
O-1/5	Radiator grille-bar—R. & R.	—	20
O-1/6	Radiator grille surround—R. & R.	—	30
O-1/7	Grille-bar badge—R. & R.	—	10
2. MOULDINGS AND BADGES			
O-2/6	Boot name badge—R. & R.	—	8
O-2/7	One wing motif—R. & R.	—	2
O-2/18	Boot motif—R. & R.	—	2
O-2/19	Bonnet name badge—R. & R.	—	8

BODY O

Operation No.		Hrs.	Mins.
3. GLASS			
O-3/1	Windscreen—R. & R.	4	30
O-3/3	One door winding window—R. & R.	—	45
O-3/7	One door winding mechanism—R. & R.	—	45
4. DOORS			
O-4/1	Rehang and adjust either door	1	0
O-4/2	Complete door assembly—R. & R.	1	0
O-4/3	One weatherstrip—R. & R.	—	30
O-4/4	One door sill plate—R. & R.	—	10
O-4/5	One trim pad—R. & R.	—	10
O-4/6	One trim pad retainer (clip)—R. & R.	—	10
O-4/7	One exterior door handle assembly—R. & R.	—	25
O-4/8	One door lock—R. & R.	—	23

BODY O

Operation No.	5. BONNET	Hrs. Mins.
O-5/1	Adjust alignment ...	– 15
O-5/2	One hinge assembly—R. & R. ...	– 35
O-5/3	Two hinge assemblies—R. & R. ...	1 0
O-5/4	Complete bonnet—R. & R. ...	– 30
O-5/5	Bonnet lock assembly—R. & R. ...	– 30
O-5/6	Adjust bonnet lock ...	– 5
	6. BOOT	
O-6/1	Adjust alignment ...	– 15
O-6/2	Complete hood assembly—R. & R. ...	1 0
O-6/3	One hinge—R. & R. ...	– 15
O-6/6	Boot lock assembly—R. & R. ...	– 30

BODY O

Operation No.	7. TRIM	Hrs. Mins.
O-7/10	One seat assembly—R. & R. ...	– 30
O-7/13	Interior rear view mirror—R. & R. ...	– 5
O-7/14	One interior sun visor—R. & R. ...	– 10

ACCESSORIES R

ROOTES SPECIAL ACCESSORIES

Operation No.		Hrs.	Mins.
R-1/2	Heater blower kit—install	–	45
R-1/3	Radio—Radiomobile—install	3	0
R-1/4	Radio—Pye—install	3	0
R-1/5	Radio—Ekco—install	3	0
R-1/8	Ammeter—install	–	30
R-1/10	Badge bar—install	–	30
R-1/11	Driving/fog lamp (1 hour for 2 units)—install	–	30
R-1/13	Windscreen washer (electric)—install	2	15
R-1/14	Safety belts (per pair) Diagonal and lap strap—install	1	0
R-1/15	Safety belts (per pair) 3-point—install	1	10
R-1/16	Door mirror—install	–	45
R-1/17	Wing mirror—install	–	15
R-1/18	Electric clock—install	–	45
R-1/19	Cigar lighter—install	–	45
R-1/30	Rimfinishers (per set)—install	–	30
R-1/31	Wheel trims (per set)—install	–	30

ACCESSORIES R

Rootes Special Accessories—continued

Operation No.		Hrs.	Mins.
R-1/32	Radiator blind—install	2	0
R-1/33	Bonnet motif—install	–	30
R-1/37	Under bonnet light—install	–	30
R-1/38	Luggage grid	–	10
R-1/41	Reverse lights—install	1	30
R-1/48	Hardtop—install	2	30
R-1/64	Oil cooler—install	0	00

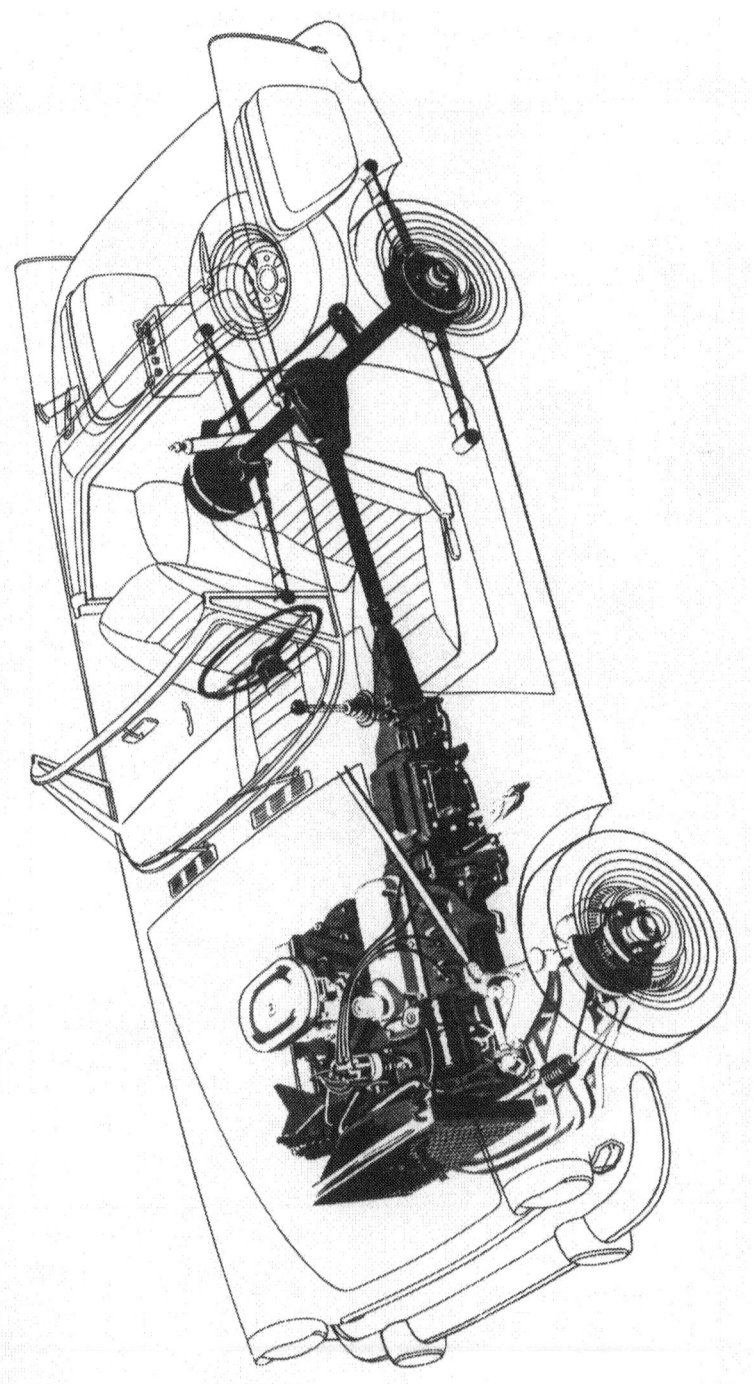

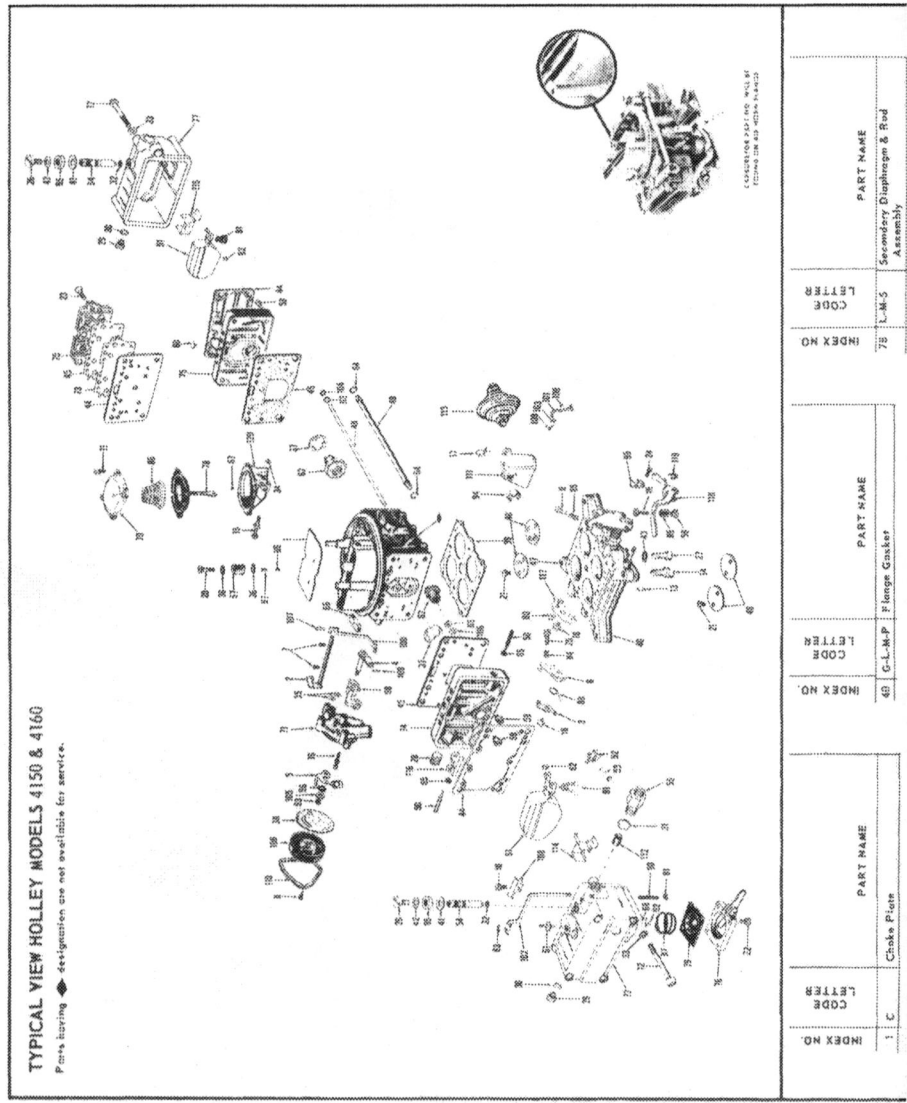

#	Code	Description
2	C	Choke Shaft Assembly
3	T	Fast Idle Pick-Up Lever
4	R	Choke Housing Shaft & Lever Assembly
5	R	Choke Thermostat Lever, Link & Piston Assembly
6	T	Fast Idle Cam Lever
7	C-L-M	Choke Plate Screws
8	L-R	Thermostat Housing Clamp Screw
9	L-T	Throttle Stop Screw
10	B-L	Air Vent Clamp Screw & Lock Washer
11	L-S	Secondary Diaphragm Cover Assy. Screw & Lock Washer
12	L	Fuel Bowl To Primary / Main Body Screw Secondary
13	L-Y	Diaphragm Lever Adjusting Screw
14	L-S	Throttle Body Screw & Lock Washer
15	L-S	Diaphragm Housing Assembly Screw & Lock Washer
16	L	Choke Housing Screw & Lock Washer
17	L	Dashpot Bracket Screw & Lock Washer
18	L-T	Fast Idle Cam Lever & Diaphragm Assembly Screw & Lock Washer
19	L-T	Pump Lever Adjusting Screw
20	L	Pump Discharge Nozzle Screw
21	L-M-T	Primary & Secondary Throttle Plate Screw
22	B-L	Fuel Pump Cover Assembly Screw & Lock Washer
23	L	Secondary Metering Body Screw
24	L-Y	Pump Cam Lock Screw
25	L-T	Fast Idle Cam Lever Adjusting Screw
26	B-L	Fuel Valve Seat Lock Screw
29	B-L	Fuel Level Check Plug
30	B-G-M-P	Fuel Level Check Plug Gasket
31	B-G-M-P	Fuel Inlet Fitting Gasket
32	B-G-M-P	Fuel Valve Seat "O" Ring Seal
33	G-M-P	Fuel Bowl Screw Gasket
34	G-M-P-S	Secondary Diaphragm Housing Gasket
35	G-M-P-R	Choke Housing Gasket
36	G-M-P	Pump Discharge Nozzle Gasket
37	G-M-P	Power Valve Body Gasket
38	G-M-P-R	Choke Thermostat Housing Gasket
39	G-M-P-T	Throttle Body Gasket
41	B-G-M-T	Fuel Valve Seat Adjusting Nut Gasket
42	B-G-M-P	Fuel Valve Seat Lock Screw Gasket
44	B-G-M-P	Fuel Bowl Gasket
45	B-G-M-P	Metering Body Gasket Primary & Secondary
46	T	Primary & Secondary Throttle Plate
47	T	Throttle Body & Shaft Assembly
48	L	Balance Tube
49	L	Fuel Line Tube
50	L-M	Idle Adjusting Needle
51	B-L	Primary & Secondary Float & Hinge Assembly
52	B	Float Hinge Adapter
53	B	Float Lever Shaft
54	B-L-M-P	Fuel Inlet Valve & Seat Assembly
55	B-L	Fuel Inlet Fitting
56	L-T	Pump Lever Adjusting Fitting
57	L-M	Pump Discharge Nozzle
58	L	Main Jet - Secondary
59	L	Main Jet - Primary
60	L	Bowl Vent Valve
61	B-L	Air Vent Valve
62	L-M-P	Power Valve Assembly - Primary
63	B-G-M-P	Balance Tube "O" Ring Seal
64	B-G-M-P	Fuel Line Tube "O" Ring Seal
65	G-M-P	Idle Needle Seal
66	C-L	Choke Rod Seal
67	L-M-S	Diaphragm Housing Check Ball
68	L-M	Pump Inlet Check Ball
69	L-M	Pump Discharge Check Ball
70	S	Secondary Diaphragm Housing Cover
71	R	Choke Housing & Plugs Assembly
72	B	Fuel Bowl Assembly Complete - Primary
73	L	Secondary Metering Body Plate
74	L	Main Metering Body & Plugs Assembly - Primary
75	L	Main Metering Body & Plugs Assembly - Secondary
76	B-L	Fuel Pump Cover Assembly
77	B	Fuel Bowl Assembly Complete - Secondary
79	B-L-M-P	Diaphragm Assembly
80	L-M-S-T	Secondary Diaphragm Link Retainer
81	B-L-M	Air Vent Rod Spring Retainer
82	B-L-M	Float Retainer
83	B-L-M	Air Vent Valve Retainer
84	L-T	Fast Idle Cam Lever Screw Spring
85	L-T	Throttle Stop Screw Spring
86	L-S	Secondary Diaphragm Spring
87	B-L	Diaphragm Return Spring
88	L-T	Fast Idle Cam Lever Spring
89	L-T	Pump Lever Adjusting Spring
90	B-L	Air Vent Rod Spring
91	B-L	Float Spring
92	L-M	Pump Check Ball Retainer Spring
93	L-R	Choke Thermostat Shaft Nut
94	L	Dashpot Nut
95	B-L	Fuel Valve Seat Adjusting Nut
96	L-R	Choke Thermostat Lever Spacer
97	L-M	Pump Discharge Needle Valve
98	L-R	Fast Idle Cam Assembly
99	L-T	Pump Cam
100	C	Choke Rod
101	T	Throttle Connecting Rod
102	B-L	Air Vent Push Rod
103	L-T	Throttle Connecting Rod Washer
104	B-L	Balance Tube Washer
105	L-R	Choke Shaft Nut Lock Washer
106	L-R	Thermostat Housing Assembly - Complete
107	C-L-M-R	Choke Rod Retainer
108	B-L	Air Vent Rod Clamp
109	L-M-T	Throttle Connecting Rod Cotter Pin
110	R	Thermostat Housing Clamp
111	L	Dashpot Bracket
112	B-L-M	Filter Spring
113	L	Dashpot Assembly
114	B	Baffle Plate - Primary
115	B	Baffle Plate - Secondary
116	T	Metering Body Vent Baffle
117	T	Diaphragm Lever Retainer
118	T	Pump Operating Lever
119	L	Pump Operating Lever Retainer
120	S	Secondary Diaphragm Housing
11	L	Heat Tube Ferrule
11	L	Accelerator Rod Retainer
11	L	Air Cleaner Stud (Long)
11	L	Choke Heat Tube

B - Bowl Kit C - Choke Shaft Kit G - Gasket Kit L - Loose Service M - Master Kit P - Pop Kit R - Choke Kit S - Secondary Diaphragm Assembly Kit
T - Throttle Body and Shaft Assembly Kit

THE SUNBEAM TIGER II

A new Sunbeam Tiger II 289 will be announced as a mid-1967 model. The majority of the changes between the Tiger 260 and the Tiger II are in the engine department. The 260 c.i.d. V-8 of the Tiger I is replaced with a 289 c.i.d. V-8.

All of the methods of increasing the power and performance of the Tiger I 260 will apply to the Tiger II 289. The LAT-1 induction kit, the LAT-20 camshaft kit are completely interchangeable, as are the majority of the other Sunbeam options.

However, the specifications of the Tiger II 289 are considerably different to those of the Tiger 260.

The LAT-1 kit supplied for the Tiger II 289 will have the Holley 1-14 four-bbl. carburetor in place of the smaller Holley 1-12 supplied for the Tiger 260. The Holley R-3259-AAS 715 c.f.m. four-bbl. will still be the hi-performance or competition option carburetor.

The Tiger II will be able to use a higher-lift camshaft than the Tiger 260 for all-out competition.

Basic specifications of the Tiger II 289 are as follow.

289 CUBIC-INCH V-8

SPECIFICATIONS FOR THE SUNBEAM TIGER II 289

ENGINE	V-8 O.H.V.
B.H.P.	200 B.H.P. @ 4400 r.p.m.
Max. torque	282 lbs. @ 2400 r.p.m.
Bore	4.005"
Stroke	2.87"
Displacement	289 cubic inches
Compression ratio	Maximum: 9.3:1
Cylinder head c.c.	Minimum: 47 c.c.
Min. deck clearance	0.015"
Camshaft timing	Intake Opens 16° BTC
	Exhaust Opens 52° BBC
	Intake Closes 70° ABC
	Exhaust Closes 24° ATC
	Overlap: Intake 40°
	Overlap: Exhaust 40°
	Duration: Intake 266°
	Duration: Exhaust 256°

Valves	Head diam.	Intake 1.788"
		Exhaust 1.457"
	Lift	Intake 0.3684" @ 0 lash
		Exhaust 0.380" @ 0 lash

Lifter type	Hydraulic tappets
Valve springs	
Intake: Outer valve closed	71-79 lbs. @ 1.78"
Exhaust: Outer valve closed	71-79 lbs. @ 1.78"
Intake: Outer valve open	166-177 lbs. @ 1.39"
Exhaust: Outer valve open	161-177 lbs. @ 1.39"
Carburetor	Single two-bbl. Ford C6DF-E

The cylinders should be hand-honed to a "cross-hatch" pattern for early and correct ring seating.

The use of a dial indicator is required to check bore size after any rebore or honing operation. Stock bore size for the 260 Tiger is 3.803".

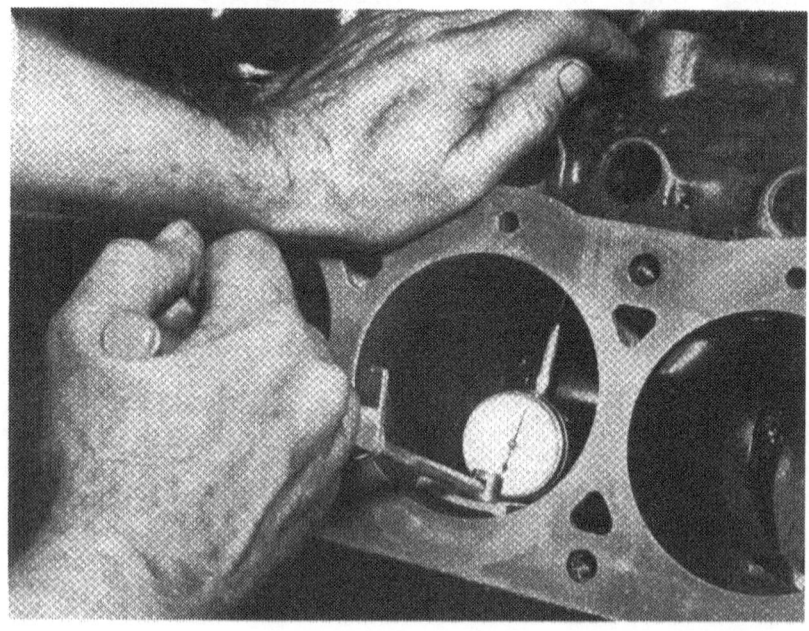

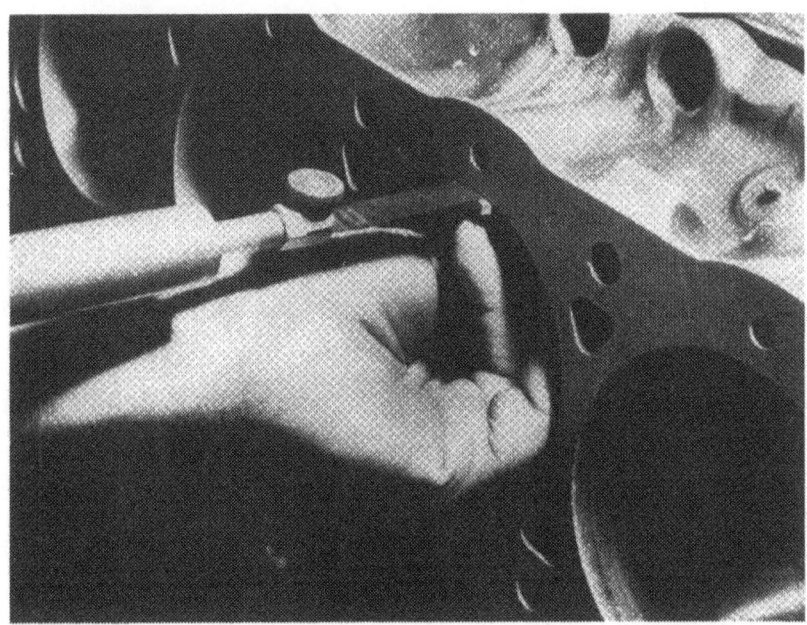

The piston-to-bore clearance is checked with the use of a "Ribbon" gauge. (See chart at the back of the book for clearance sizes.)

Deck height (distance from top of piston at TDC to top of cylinder block) is checked with a dial indicator; minimum height is .010" for a competition engine. All pistons must have the exact deck height.

Check the area around the piston skirt and crankshaft throws for clearance; mark and remove any metal from the piston skirt before having the pistons and crankshaft balanced.

When assembling the connecting rods, pistons, and crankshaft unit, slip a piece of plastic tube over the rod bolts to prevent damage to the crankshaft bearing areas.

When installing a new camshaft, or when re-assembling an engine, always use a new timing chain and timing gears.

After installation of a new camshaft, install right side cylinder head and turn the engine through by hand to check for valve-to-piston clearance.

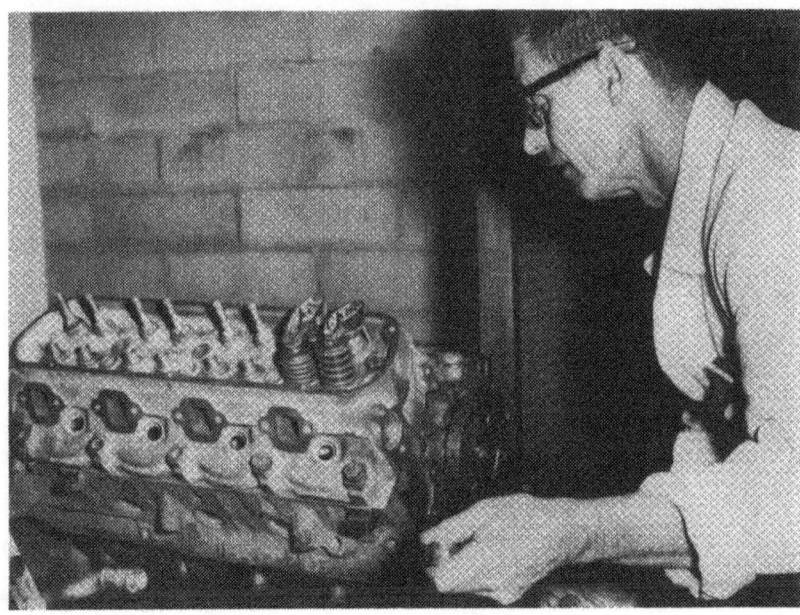

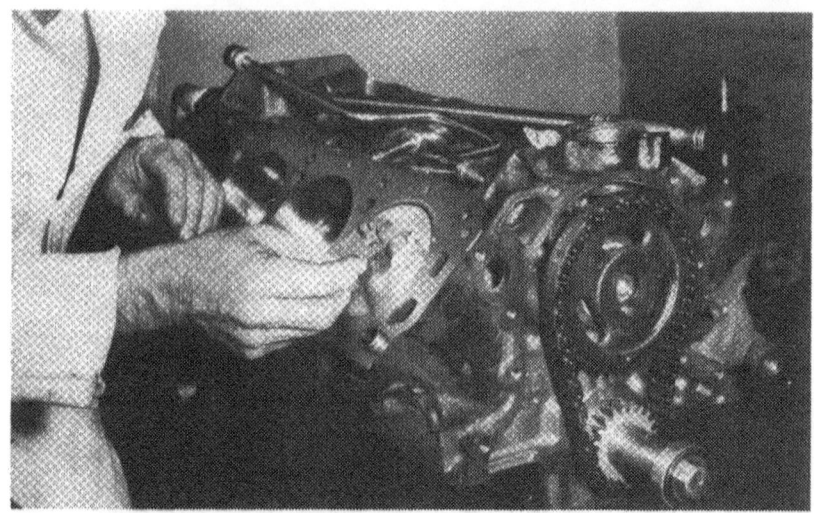

The valve-to-piston clearance is checked by filling the valve pockets in the pistons with modeling clay. After turning the engine through by hand as shown in picture #9.E., carefully remove the head, cut the modeling clay in half and carefully remove the clay from one side of the pocket. Using a dial indicator, measure the distance between the valve and the piston. It is important that there is a minimum of .080"; however, a clearance of .125" is preferable.

Stock flat-top pistons (left); JE- flat-top pistons with valve pockets or "fly-cuts" (right).

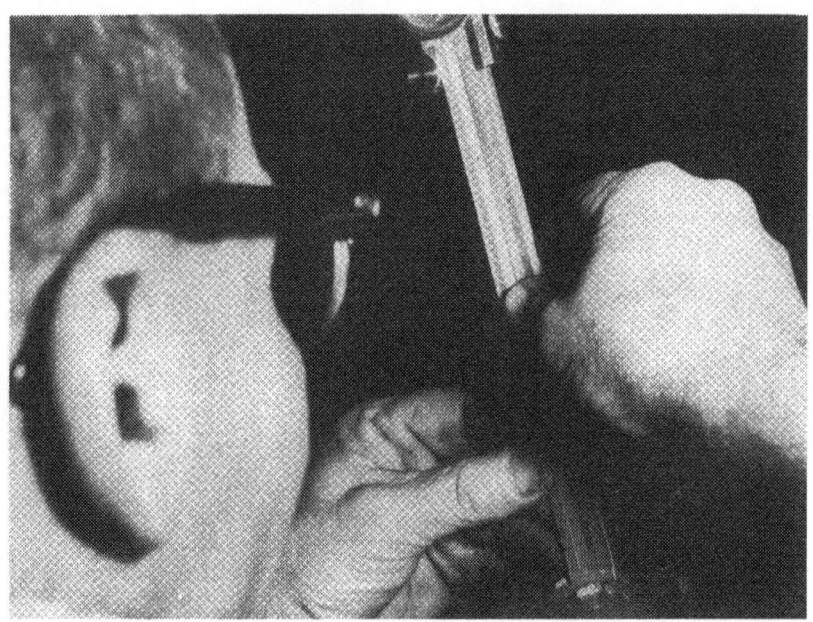

The valve pocket or fly-cut is very important if a high-lift type camshaft is going to be used.

If using the standard flat-top pistons, and the LAT-20 camshaft and the 289 c.i.d. cylinder heads with the larger 1.788" intake valves, the intake valve area will have to be fly-cut in the stock piston. This is not required if the LAT-20 camshaft is used with the stock 260 c.i.d. cylinder heads and the stock 1.67" intake valves.

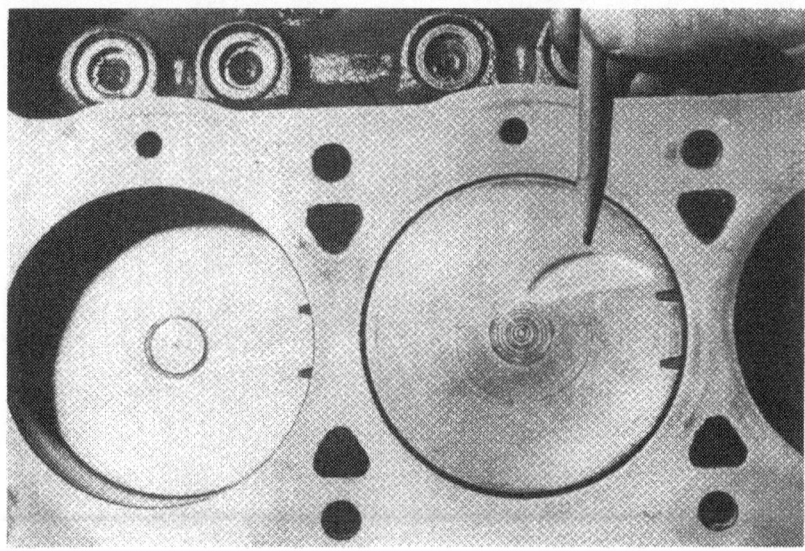

For all-out competition road racing or modified sports car classes the use of the JE "deflector-wedge" or "Pop-top" pistons will be required to gain maximum compression ratios. Note that the valve areas have relieved flat spots to prevent piston to valve interference.

The Tiger-260 uses a block that is identified by the three (3) freeze plugs on the side, whereas a Ford Falcon 260 block will only have two (2) freeze plugs.

With the cylinder heads removed, the Tiger-260 block can be identified by the almost straight line across the top of the block; this block can be used with the .030" "thin" steel head gaskets to increase the compression ratio.

The standard Ford Falcon 260 c.i.d. block; note the small "w" shape across the top. This block cannot use the thin steel .030" head gasket, but must use only the standard Ford 260 cylinder head gasket.

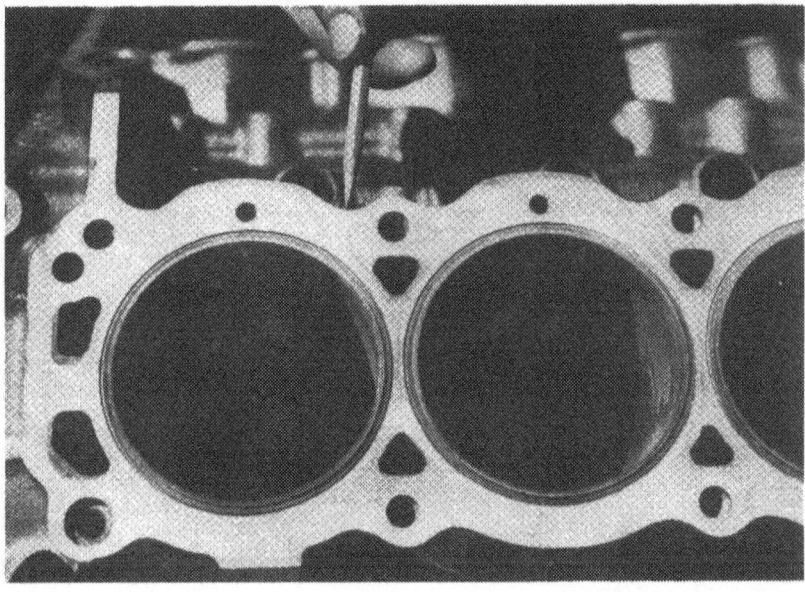

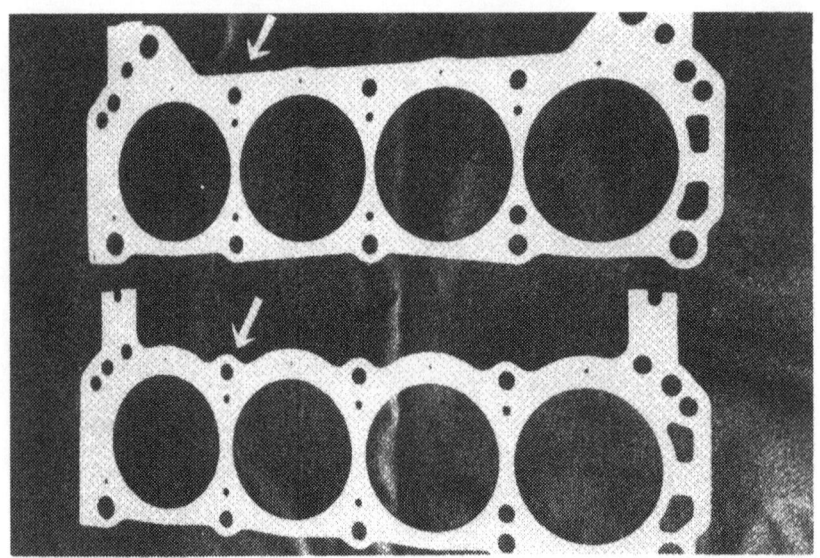

Difference between the standard 260 "heavy" cylinder head gasket shown on bottom. This stock gasket is .070" thick.
The "thin" steel 289 cylinder head gasket which is .030" thick, shown on the top, can be used only on the special Tiger block.

When assembling the engine, attention must be paid to the correct torquing figures listed in the back of the book.

A fully degreed crankshaft pulley is advisable on any competition engine and the standard pulley can be degreed by any good machine shop.

The stock generator pulley shown here is too small for competition engines and can cause thrown fan belts.

The optional pulley (Ford part #C30Z-10130-B) should be installed on any Tiger that is using a low gear final drive (high numbered). This pulley, larger than standard, will reduce the generator-to-crankshaft pulley ratios over 50% and reduce the possibility of thrown fan belts at high engine rpm's. With this pulley, use an "Atlas #727" fan belt.

The 245 B.H.P. 260 c.i.d. Tiger complete. Note that the carburetor is shown without an air-horn or filter. It should not be run this way. The Holley requires some form of air-straightener over its air horn.

The 289 c.i.d. heads shown on top; the 260 c.i.d. heads shown on bottom.

The stock "pressed-in" rocker arm studs of the 260 c.i.d. heads must be replaced with "screw-in" type rocker arm studs for high rpm operations.

The 289 c.i.d. heads with screw-in studs and valve spring valley shown on left; the 260 stock heads shown on right.

The use of a hand tap is required to thread the stock 260 heads for use with the screw-in rocker arm studs.

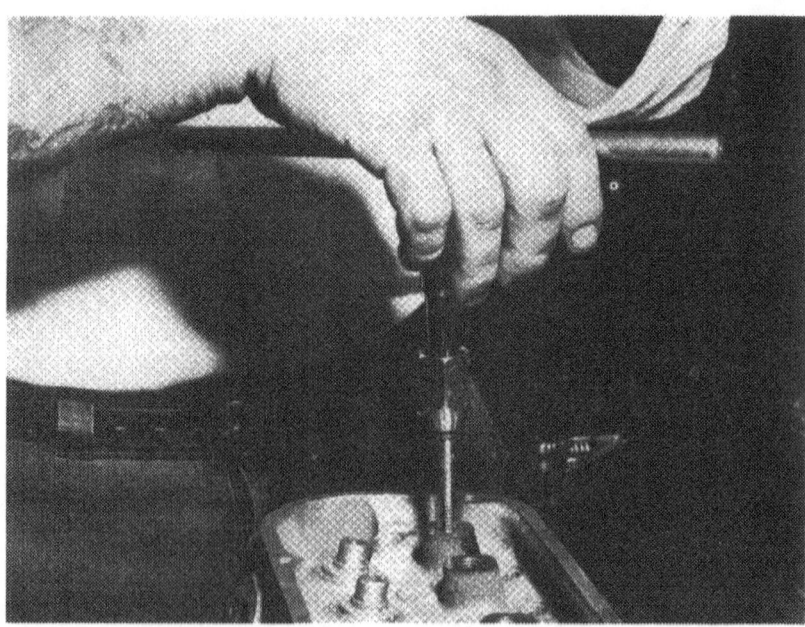

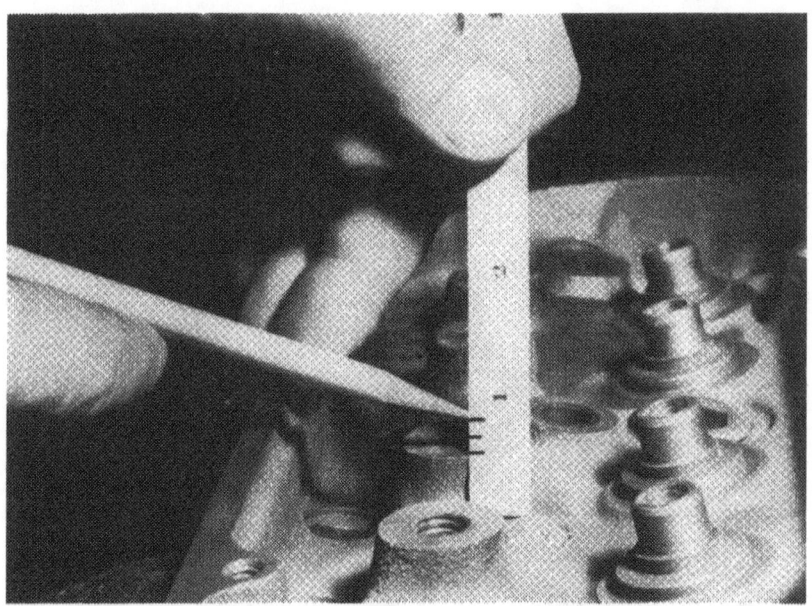

Approximately ¼″ must be removed from the rocker stud boss to correct the required 1.60:1 ratio of the rocker arms when modifying the stock head to take screw-in studs.

Use care when removing any carbon from the valve pockets.

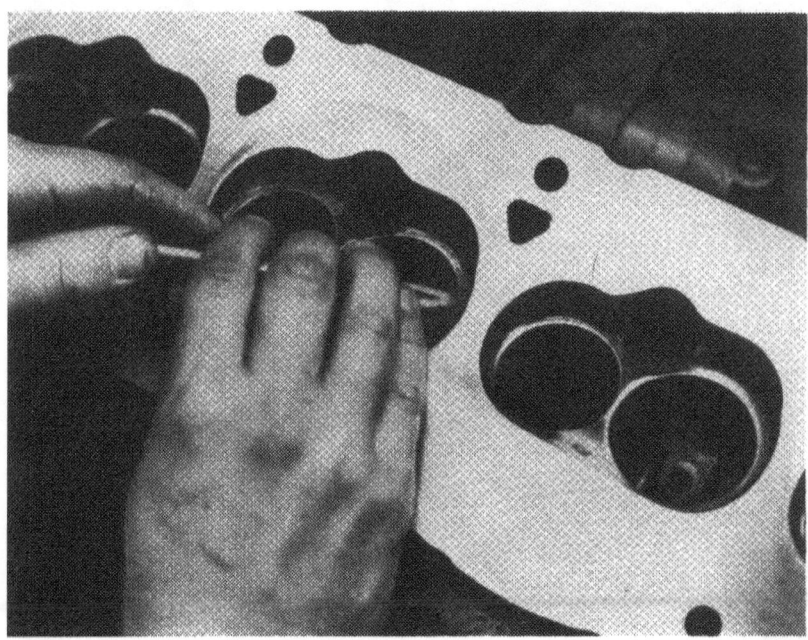

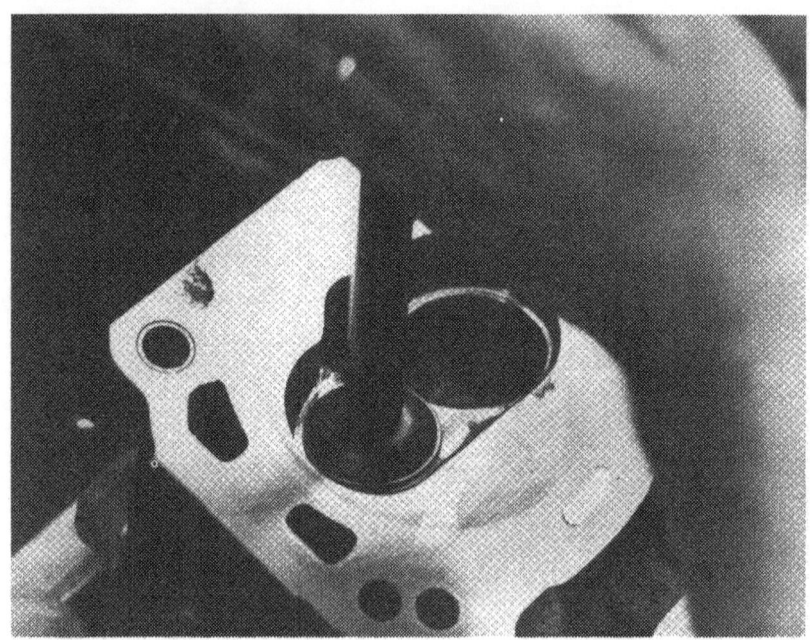

Valves should be hand-lapped for correct fit.

Constant checking is required on racing valve jobs.

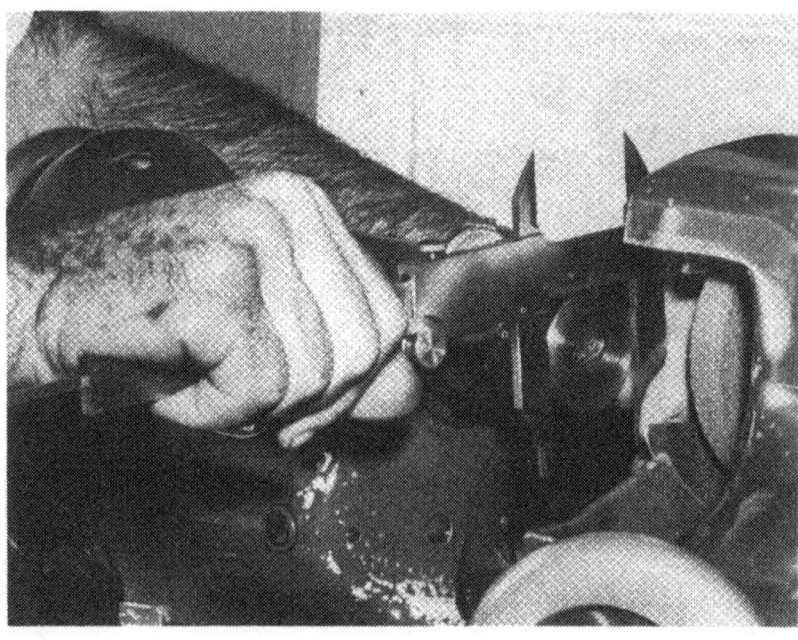

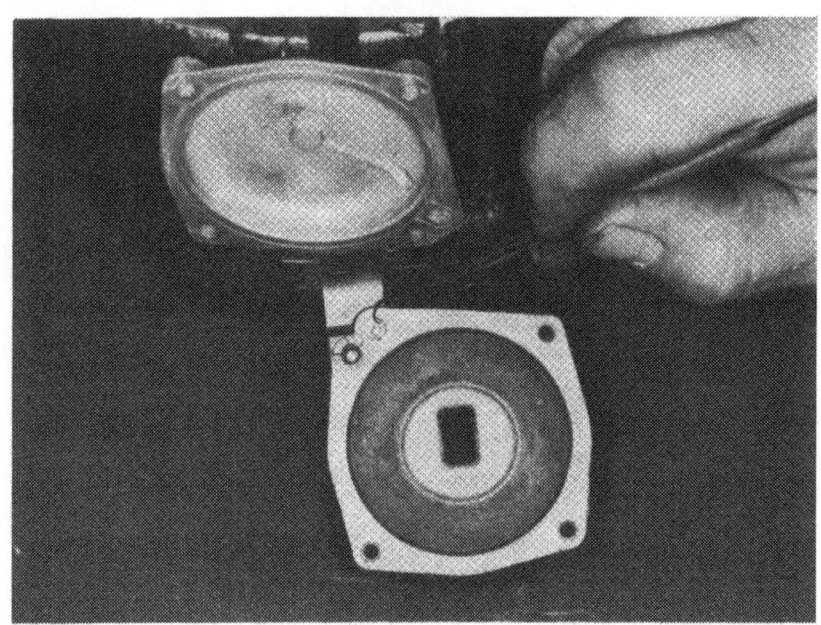

Stock Holley 4-bbl. carb. vacuum diaphragm, check-ball seat pointed out; this is the view you will see with the check-ball removed.

Using a small Phillips-head type screwdriver and small ball-peen hammer, lightly tap the screwdriver into the check-ball seat opening to enlarge the opening as shown. This will allow the secondary throttles to open approximately 30% faster than normal.

The Holley jets can be checked for approximate sizes by the use of small numbered wire drills. They should not, however, be re-drilled to enlarge their sizes unless as an emergency step. Then they should be remarked as to their new opening sizes.

Float levels are first made dry with the float bowls removed and inverted. The final adjustment is to be made on the engine using the visual sight plugs with the engine running at warm idle.

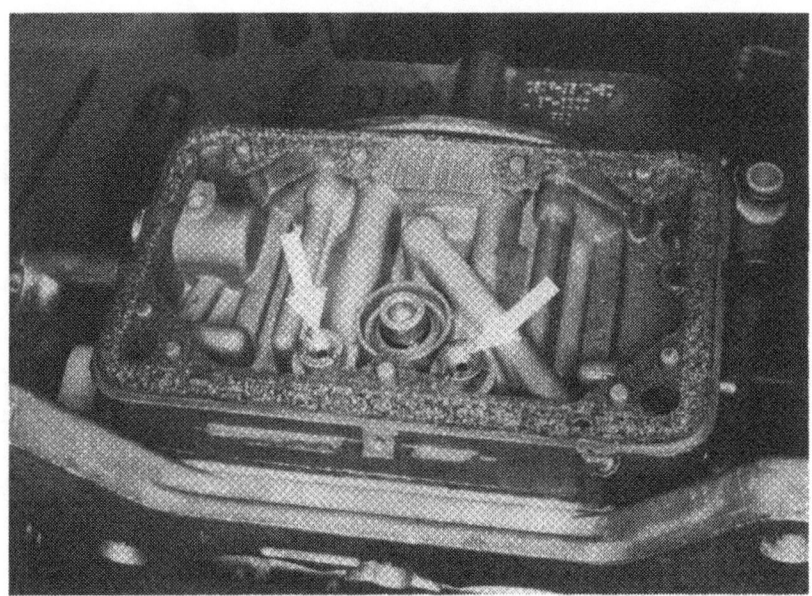

Metering jet body shown with a set of "screw-in" type jets used in the primary system of the Holley 1-1.2 and the primary and secondary systems of the Holley R-3259 carburetors.

For cars that are being set up for maximum acceleration use, it is sometimes necessary to have a set of small tubes silver-soldered into the openings of the jets to prevent fuel from running away from the jets under hard acceleration.

The smaller Holley 1-12 4-bbl. carburetor uses a main-jet metering plate in the secondary system in place of the metering jet body shown in pictures 36.C. and 37.C. To change the jetting of the secondary system where this plate is used, the entire plate is changed. Larger numbered plates are richer; i.e., stock jet plate is # 2007-3. One step richer would be a # 2007-4, two steps richer, # 2007-5; etc.

The stock Holley dump tubes, shown in hands, should be replaced by the longer dump tubes shown in carburetor. Make sure that when fitting new dump tubes, they are pin-fitted. The tubes must not be loose; they could work down into the throttle butterflies and cause a stuck throttle, or even work down into the valves.

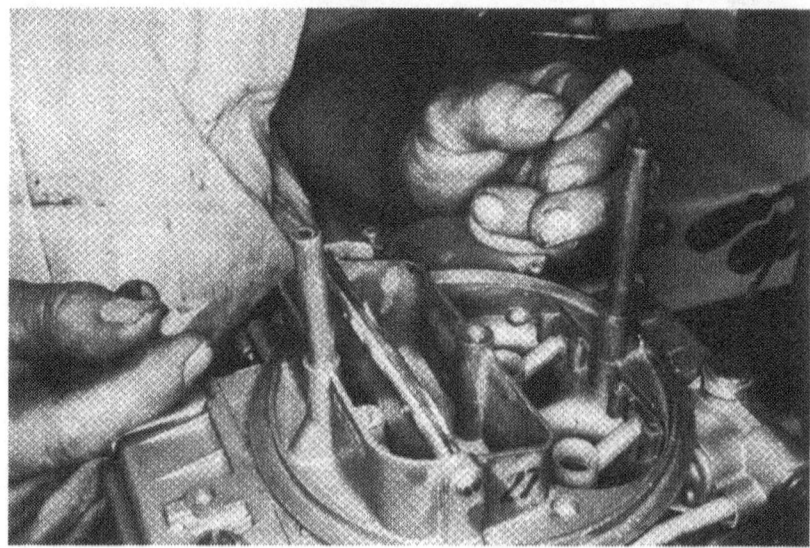

Optional LAT-1 "Hi-Rise" aluminum intake manifold and small Holley 1-12 four-bbl. carburetor.

Carburetor mounting opening of the LAT-1 Hi-Rise intake manifold. The two sets of carburetor mounting screw holes are supplied if other than a Holley carb. is to be fitted, such as a AFB.

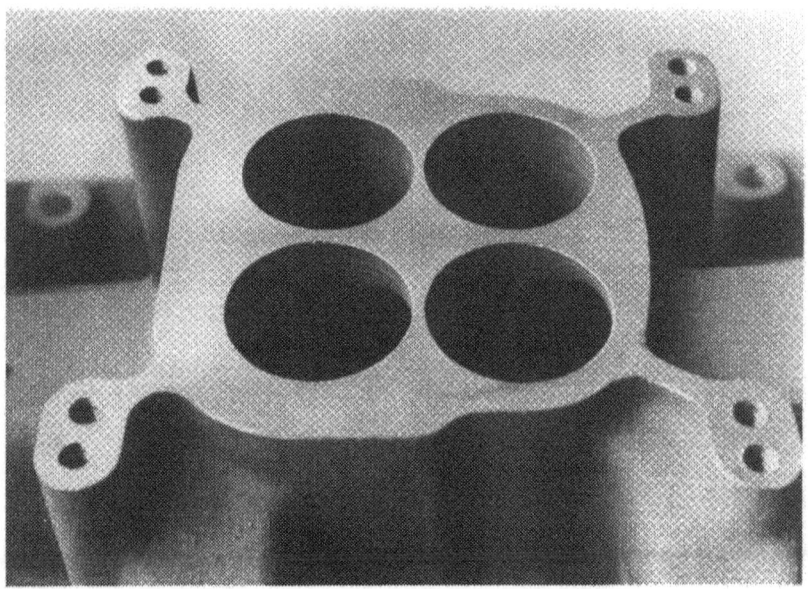

A racing modification to the intake manifold is made by removing the metal between the right side primary and secondary passages, and the left side primary and secondary passages. This will add approx. 7-15 HP at the top end. The work should be done only by a complete machine shop and should not be made with the manifold on the engine.

The stock clutch pressure plate, shown on the right and bottom. Pencil is pointing to the weak spot of the housing. Competition Hays clutch is shown on left (white unit). This type of pressure plate should be used on all competition cars.

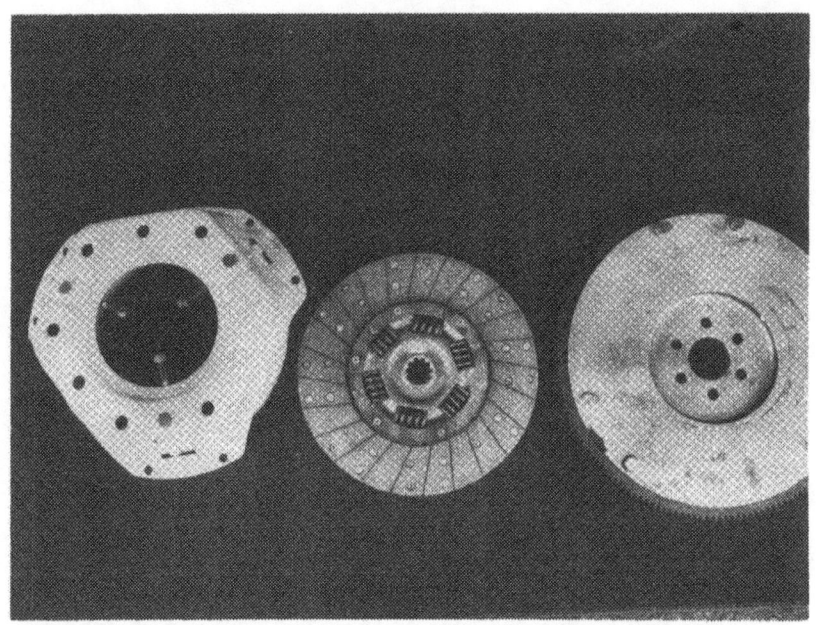

Recommended for competitions cars is the complete Hays clutch pressure plate, disc, and steel-billet flywheel, all explosion and blow-up proof units.

Hays clutch pressure plate and disc on left, compared to stock HD units on right.

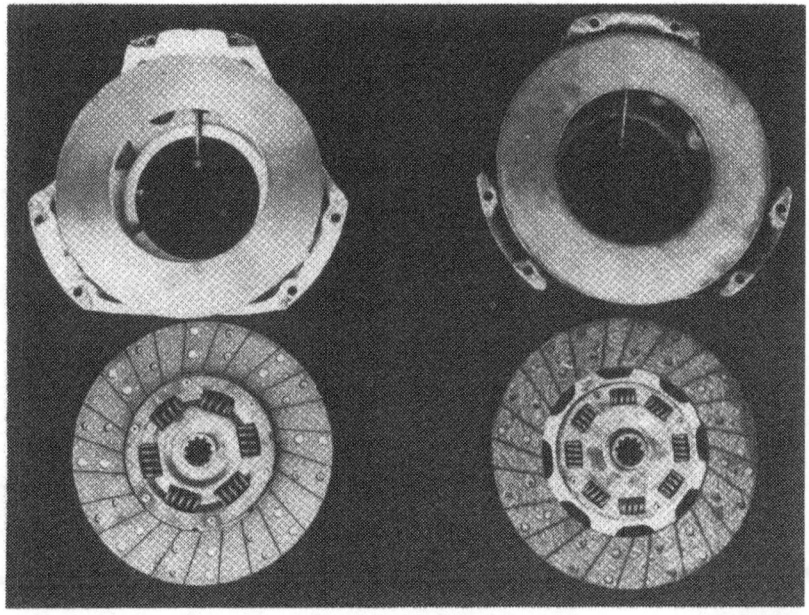

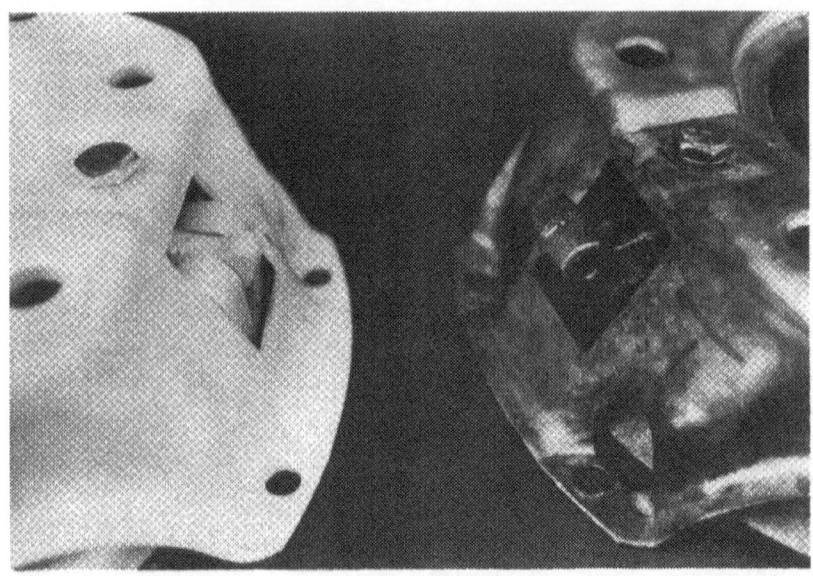

Hays pressure plate on left (white unit) showing solid housing area around fingers, also lack of counter-weights on arms. Stock HD unit on right; note heavy counter-weights on arms which prevent high rpm shifting and weak open area around mounting bolt hole.

It is recommended that the pressure-plate to flywheel mounting bolts be replaced with larger HD bolts, shown on left.

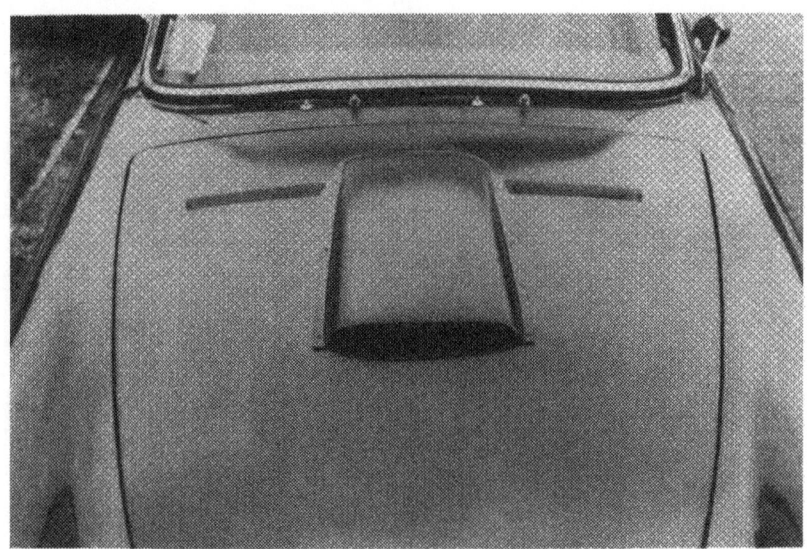

For S.C.C.A. racing events, there is an optional fiberglass hood air-scoop and cooling vents available for the stock steel hood. A side view of the hood scoop. It can be mounted by "pop-rivets" to the standard hood after first cutting a round hole, approx. 8" in diameter, directly over the carburetor area.

An inexpensive method of solving the heat problem can be the use of louvers which can be done by any good custom body shop. Cost is less than $10.00 plus the cost of repainting the hood, which will be required. Louvers should be in a direct line over the exhaust manifolds.

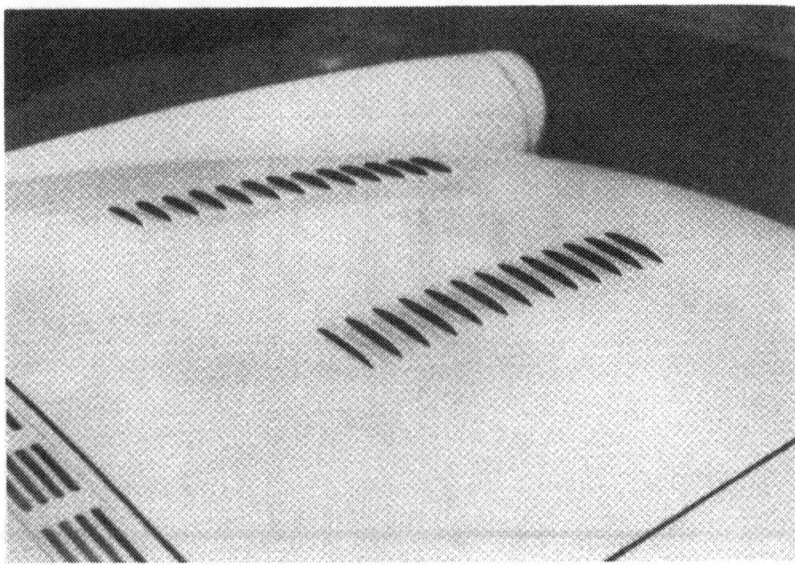

The best choice for the Tiger is the use of the LAT-79 fiberglass hood. It has a built-in fresh air intake scoop plus engine heat exhaust vents. While it comes with square rear corners they can be trimmed off to fit early Tigers.

The LAT-5, Traction-Master kit should be considered a must for every Tiger. It will prevent the rear spring wrapping up under hard acceleration, and help the braking as well.

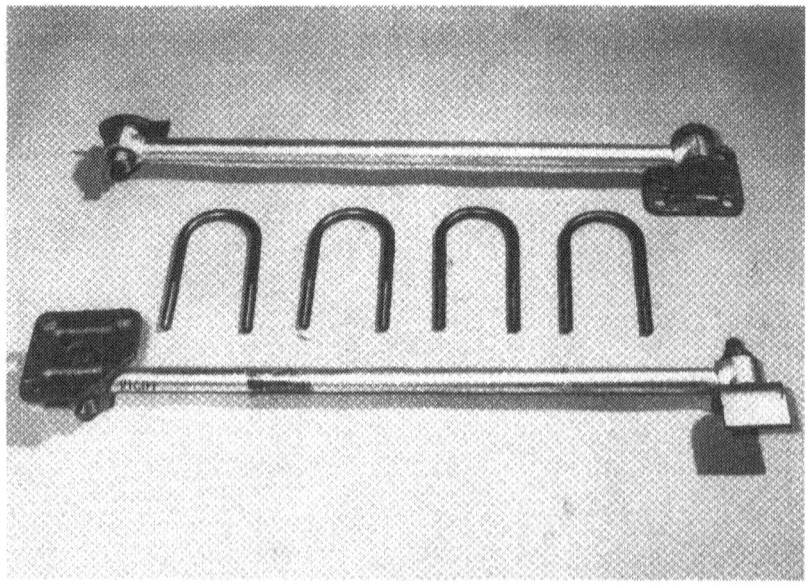

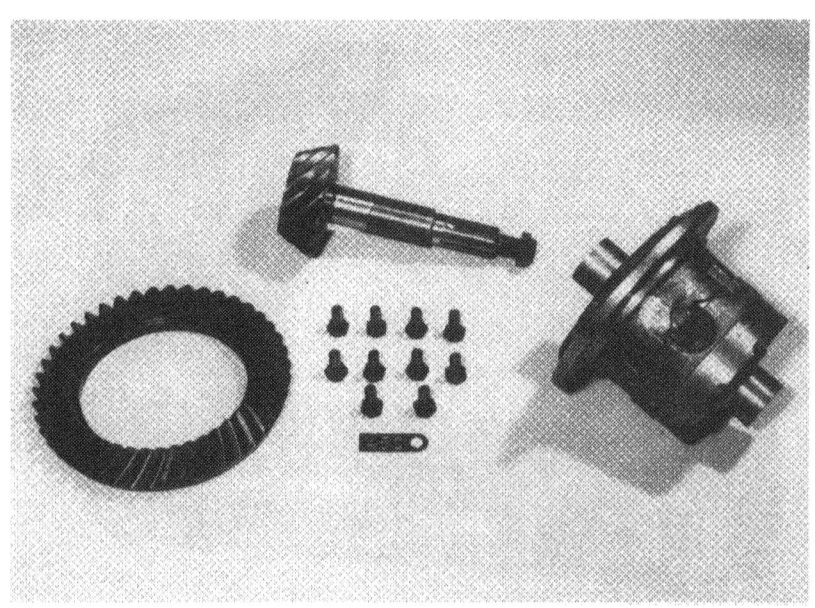

The LAT-50, limited slip, shown here with the LAT-54; 3.73:1 final drive ratio should be used for competition; rally, and trails service cars. Ratios are available from 3.07:1 up to 3.73:1.

The LAT-74 two-inch low restriction exhaust system will offer improved performance for road use cars.

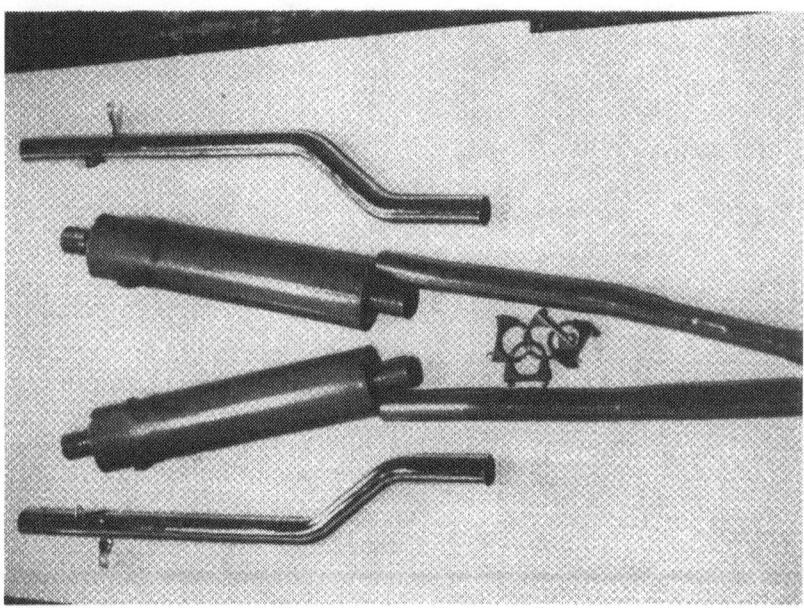

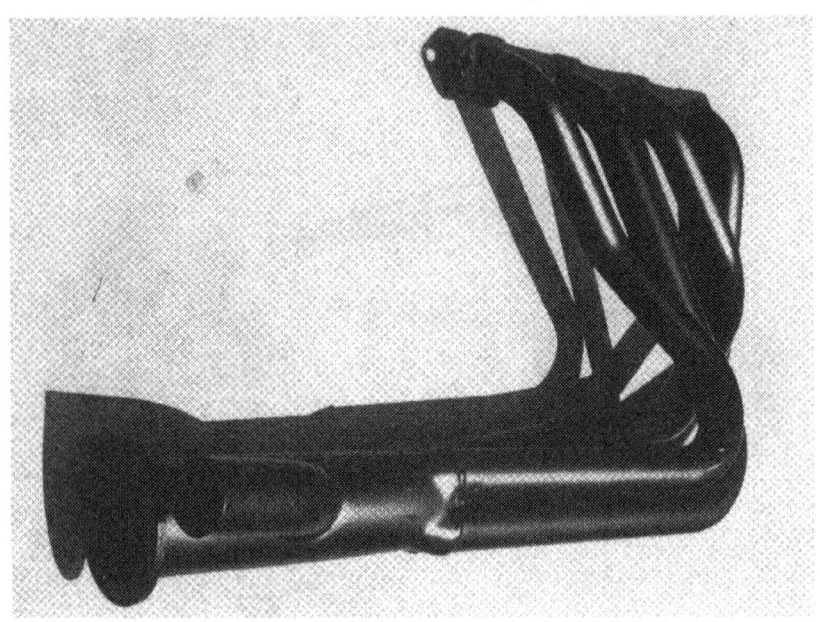

The LAT-73 competition headers are recommended for competition use, but will offer improved performance for the hotter street machines.

The LAT-73 header installed on the Tiger. No body work is required to fit these headers.

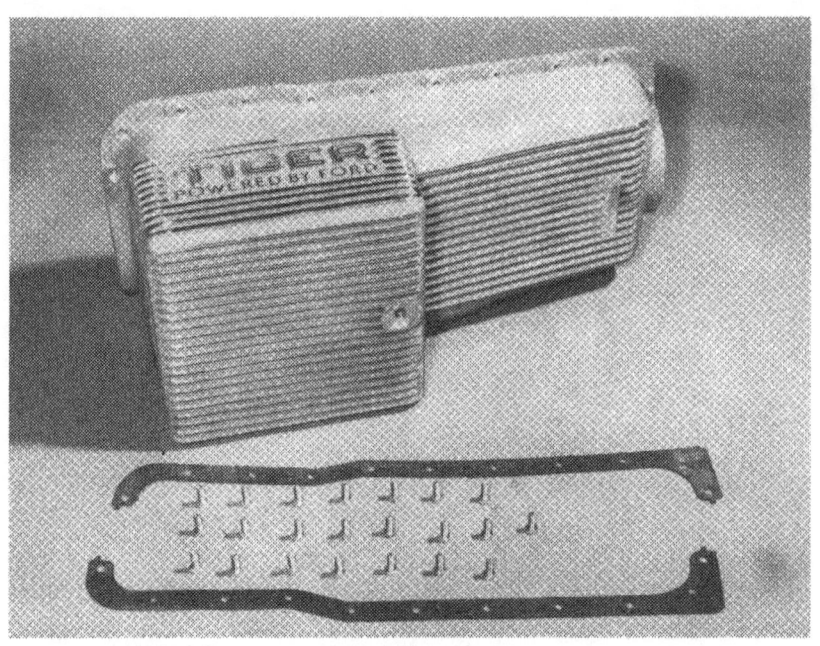

The LAT-4 is a finned, large capacity, aluminum oil pan.

For racing, the high carbon steel scatter-shield is a requirement. It is approved for both N.H.R.A., A.H.R.A. and S.C.C.A. competition use.

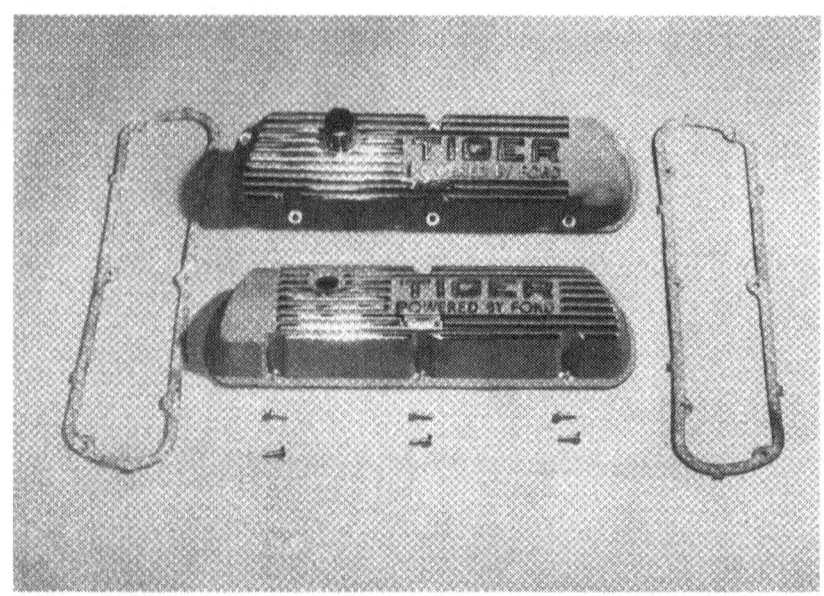

The LAT-8 cast aluminum valve covers add appearance to under the Tiger's hood, and are specially made with the rear fin area removed to prevent interference under the fire wall.

The LAT-20 camshaft kit come complete with solid lifter camshaft, new tappets valve springs, gaskets, and a dual-point distributor. It will fit all Tiger 260s and the new Tiger II, 289.

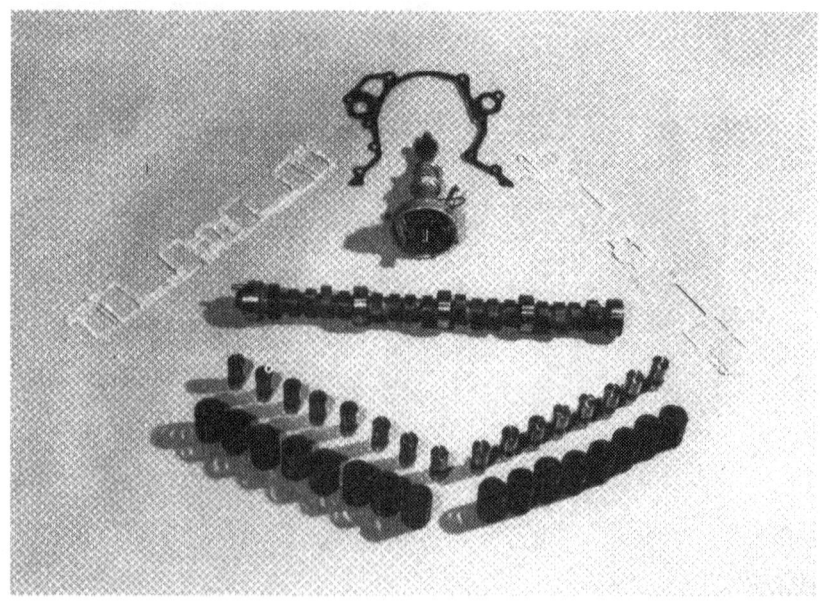

The Sunbeam removable hard-top offers complete weather protection, and the quarter-windows open for flow-thru ventilation.

When the LAT-20 kit is installed, it is useful to add the LAT-22, 0-7000 rpm tach.

The use of a **P&G** valve gapping tool is to be recommended for the solid lifter cammed Tigers.

A fender cover will protect the Tigers finish when working on the engine.

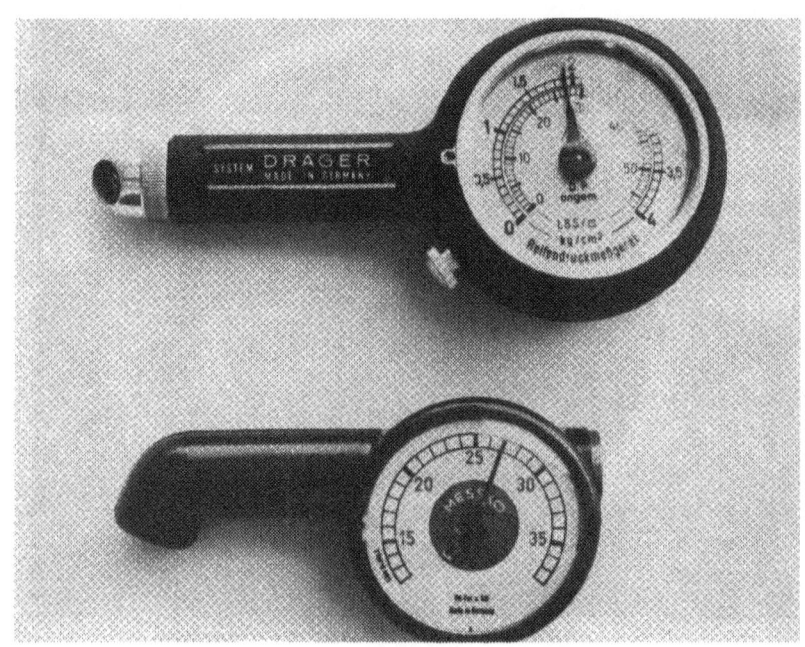

An accurate tire gauge should be in every Tiger's tool box.

For rallye fans a lap clipboard with stop watch holders will be handy.

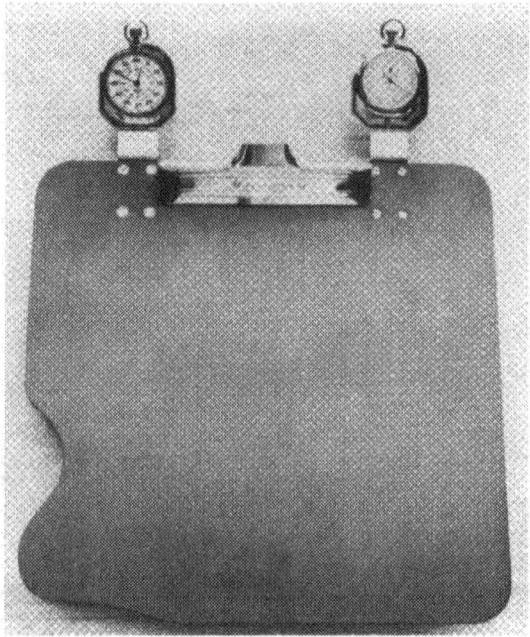

A leather steering wheel cover will add a slight amount of thickness to the Tiger's wheel, and offers a firm grip.

Lucas hi-speed driving lights can be used only in some states, but the fog lights are legal everywhere. Can be bumper-mounted.

The LAT-70 aluminum wheel is recommended for street use. Its size is 5.5x13" as compared to the stock steel wheel, which is 4.5x13".

For racing use, American Racing Equipment has magnesium racing wheels available in sizes up to 6.5x13 for the Tigers.

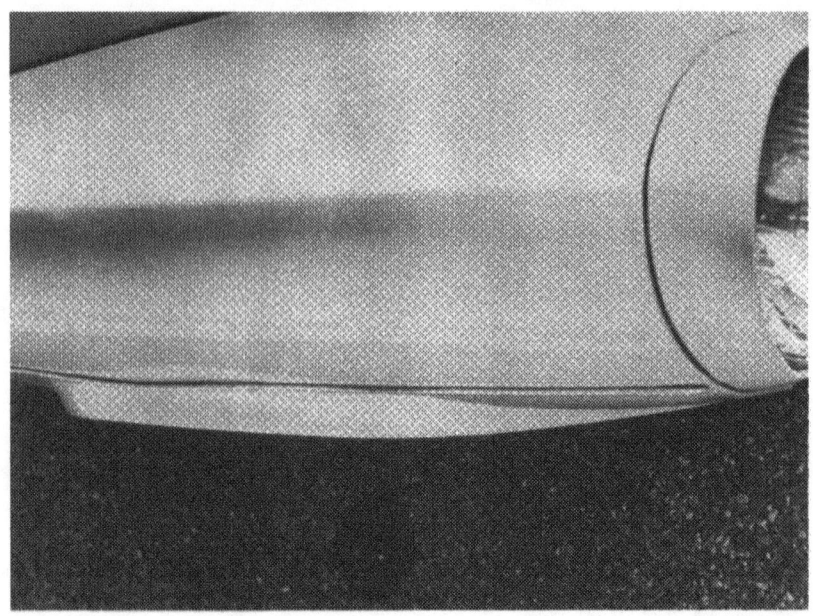

It is sometimes necessary to flare out the fenders to clear racing tires. Front shown from above.

Rear fender flared for racing tires.

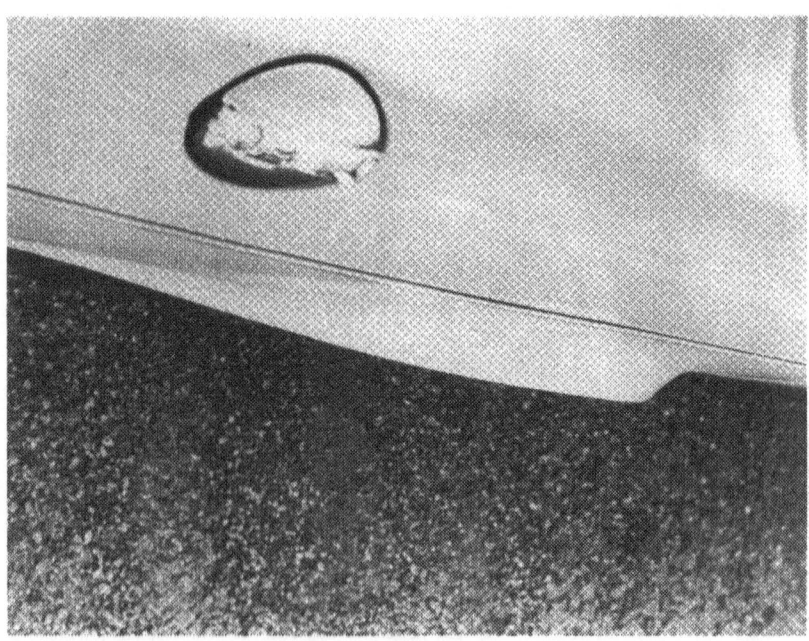

The largest two-bbl. carburetor that will fit on the stock Tiger intake manifold is the Holley 1-45., 350 c.f.m.

The author driving the Larry Reed Sports Cars Drag racing Sunbeam Tiger. It has hit a top speed of 108.00 mph in the standing start ¼-mile, in just 12.95 seconds elapsed time.

Ron Dykes, driving the Riverside GP B-Production Class winning Sunbeam Tiger of Vincent Motors.

Ahead of every other B/P car at the 1966 Riverside GP, Ron Dykes finished 1st in Class (B/P) and 4th overall in the A and B race for production Sports Cars. The Tiger hit speeds of up to 157 mph on the straight.

The author, during a A.H.R.A. Record run.

The stock 260 c.i.d., 164 BHP Tiger engine with normal engine compartment layout.

Left side of stock 164 BHP Tiger engine. Note the vacuum distributor and radio carbon ignition wires.

www.ingramcontent.com/pod-product-compliance
Lightning Source LLC
Chambersburg PA
CBHW020126240426
43673CB00038B/607